STARTUP BOARDS

STARTUP

BOARDS

GETTING THE MOST OUT OF
YOUR BOARD OF DIRECTORS

BRAD FELD
MAHENDRA RAMSINGHANI

WILEY

ISBN 9781118443668 (Hardcover)
ISBN 9781118516843 (ePDF)
ISBN 9781118516829 (ePub)

Printed in the United States of America
V10014115_091919

CONTENTS

FOREWORD

The phone rang at the appointed hour. My client, a software company CEO, was calling for his regular session. I picked up the phone.

"Hello"

"Why the hell does my board act like that?"

"Good morning, James," I answered and we both laughed.

We talked through the upcoming financing. Some of the investors—folks who came into the company only in the last round—were already jockeying around terms and prices of the upcoming round. Some of the other directors—investors who had been with the company since the beginning—were also beginning to draw a hard line around terms that they would find acceptable.

In a sense, while they were all directors, as investors they were beginning to play a game of chicken with the company's financing—each holding fast to a position deemed best for the shareholders they represent and yet, as the negotiations ticked on, the company's ability to actually raise the needed funds could be jeopardized.

After the session, I asked him if I could quote him.

"Sure," he said, "just let me know if I ever end up with an actual video recording of me calling [the board member] a 'fuckhead'—it's not that I'd be bothered by that, it's just that I'd want to make sure I sent the link to all my friends."

A year ago I was sitting in the office of the CEO of a company on whose board I served. The recently elected chair and the CEO were screaming at each other and, as usual, I found myself trying to mediate.

"What you don't understand," said the chair rising from his chair and trying to tower over the seated CEO, "is that you're here," and he held out his right hand, palm down, "and the board is here," and he moved his left hand on top of the right, again palm down, "and I'm here," and he placed his right hand over the left.

Capo dei capi—boss of bosses.

My client's question was spot on: Why does this happen? What is it that makes the relationship among board members, investors, and management so tricky? And even when you remove the notion of director as investor (or investor representative) you can still end up with troubled relations.

The board/management relationship is tricky, complex, and nuanced. There are few structures within traditional businesses that are quite like it. Most businesses, indeed most organizations, are built on some variation of a command-and-control structure. Because of their inherent hierarchical nature, it's often clear who's in charge, who makes the decisions, and who's ultimately responsible for what.

Even in businesses where the power and decision making reflects not the pyramid of classic command and control but the inverted pyramid of the ways in which information and therefore accountability should flow, there's relative clarity.

But when it comes to boards of directors, confusion is often the norm and, as a result, there's accompanying frustration and anger. For example, does the CEO work for the board of directors or the company? Does the board "work" for the company? Who holds individual board members accountable for their actions? What is the relationship between board and staff members?

Underlying all of this is the responsibility to represent the shareholders.

I've served on dozens of boards of directors—this includes public and private companies, for-profit businesses, and not-for-profit organizations. I think the core troubles stem from a misunderstanding of the key elements of the roles.

Directors aren't quite like any other management position in an organization. They have power but often lack the information to wield that power as well as managers. They have perspective—often significantly more experience than senior management—but, by the nature of their responsibility, they are disconnected from the day-to-day operations.

Directors need to remember they have a delicate balancing act of influencing without dictating, and engaging and sharing their experience and perspective by virtue of their gravitas as much as a result of their power.

Management, too, needs to remember that the task of being a director or a trustee is unlike any other job one has ever had. There's an explicit accountability that goes along with the job, and that fact, combined with the implicit lack of information, can cause most folks to feel terribly anxious and to act in awful ways.

This book by Brad Feld and Mahendra Ramsinghani will help everyone on both sides of that divide to take a needed step back, see things from the other view, and work toward making the board as functional as possible.

JERRY COLONNA
Life and Business Coach
Retired Venture Capitalist
Chair, Naropa University

ACKNOWLEDGMENTS

The original inspiration for the Startup Revolution series came from a conversation we had several years ago. Mahendra and Brad met briefly in person in Ann Arbor at an event that Brad and his partner Jason Mendelson held for *Venture Deals: Be Smarter than Your Lawyer and Venture Capitalist*. Mahendra followed up a few days later with an e-mail suggesting that we write a book about boards of directors together. A year later, a five-book series was launched, with *Startup Boards* as book number four.

This has been a challenging book to write. Both of us worked hard to cover a lot of territory, both traditional and non-traditional, without putting ourselves, and you, to sleep. We'll let you be the judge of whether we achieved this and, if you are napping, we hope you are in a comfortable position.

Many people have contributed to this book. We appreciate all the efforts, interviews, and writing from Micah Baldwin, Scott Bannister, Jacques Benkoski, Paul Berberian, Rajat Bhargava, Steve Blank, Matt Blumberg, Tom Bogan, Jeff Bussgang, Jon Callaghan, Dane Collins, Jim Dai, Greg Gottesman, Chris Heidelberger, Will Herman, Ben Horowitz, Richard Huston, Eric Jensen, Josh Kopelman, Clint Korver, Manu Kumar, Wendy Lea, Aileen Lee, Seth Levine, Scott Maxwell, T. A. McCann, Kelly McCracken, Ryan McIntyre, Jason Mendelson, Lesa Mitchell, Cindy Padnos, Mike Platt, Thomas Porter, Andy Rappaport, Christopher Rizik, Niel Robertson, Adam Rodnitzsky, Heidi Roizen, William Ruckelshaus, Lucy Sanders, Greg Sands, Zachary Shulman, Mike Smalls, Mark Solon, Mark Suster, Shanna Tellerman, Steven Tonsfeldt, Sreeram Veeragandham, Todd Vernon, Noam Wasserman, Scott Weiss, and Fred Wilson.

The team that we worked with at Wiley, especially Bill Falloon, Meg Freeborn, Tiffany Charbonier, and Sharon Polese, did a great job.

Once again, Brad's wife Amy Batchelor took out her red pen and did a great editing job on several early drafts. At a key moment in time, Jason read an early draft and helped us restructure it so it was much better. Amy also put up with a week-long trip to Miami where we hung out at the W Hotel and mostly procrastinated, which we have learned is an integral part of the writing process.

PART ONE

OVERVIEW

CHAPTER ONE

INTRODUCTION

The word *boardroom* conjures up images of important people puffing on cigars or sipping Scotch while sitting in leather chairs in wood-paneled rooms. These important people are talking about complex things that determine the future of companies. Formality and seriousness fill the air. Big decisions are being made.

While first-time chief executive officers (CEOs) and founders often have an elevated view of the boardroom, great startup boards aren't fancy, complex, or pretentious. Instead, a startup board is usually a small group of people trying to help build your company.

Over the years, we've served on hundreds of boards. A few were great, many were good, and some were terrible. When things in a company were going smoothly, the board was congratulatory and supportive. When there were challenges, some boards helped and some boards hurt. The tempo and interactions of these boards varied dramatically. In some cases reality prevailed, and in others it was denied.

In 2010, after a particularly tedious board meeting, Brad realized that the default structure of a startup board was an artifact of the past 40 years, dating back to the way early venture-backed company boards operated. Things had changed and evolved some, but the dramatic shift in communication patterns and technology over the past decade hadn't been incorporated into the way most boards worked. As a result, Brad ran a two-year experiment where he tried different things; some successful, some not. As with every experiment, he did more of what worked, modified and killed what didn't, tried new things, and measured a lot of stuff.

The idea for this book emerged during this experiment. We decided that in addition to describing the new startup board approach that resulted from Brad's experiment, it was important to lay the groundwork and explain clearly how startup boards worked, how they could be most effective, and what the challenges were. Brad's new board approach built on the traditional board of directors, so rather than throw it out, we use a highly functioning one as the basis for a new, evolved, and much more effective approach to a board of directors.

While the topic may feel dry, we've tried, as Brad and Jason Mendelson (Foundry Group, Managing Director) did in *Venture Deals: Be Smarter Than Your Lawyer and Venture Capitalist*, to take a serious topic, cover it rigorously, but do it in plain English with our own brand of humor. Our goal is to demystify how a board of directors works, discuss historical best and worst practices, and give you a clear set of tools for creating and managing an awesome board.

WHY DOES A STARTUP NEED A BOARD?

Entrepreneurs, the creators and architects of creative construction (with apologies to Schumpeter[1]), enjoy creating new products and companies from just an idea. These forceful personalities break new ground and explore uncharted territory while their unstoppable drive changes the world we live in. As a society, we should be grateful to the entrepreneurial force that creates new things, but often this new-new thing causes fear and uncertainty in the old and the established, followed by resistance and denial. Whether it is building a new product, landing the first customer, raising the initial round of capital, or recruiting early team members, an entrepreneur's journey can be lonely, stressful, and extremely challenging. While entrepreneurship currently is popular—even trendy—this is not always the case, and the journey to create a successful company can be a long and difficult one.

One of the early challenges encountered is raising money. While many startups are bootstrapped, with the founders choosing to focus on generating revenue to fund their business, other entrepreneurs choose to raise money from friends and family, angel investors, or venture capitalists (VCs). The challenges of raising the first round of capital are well documented, and only a small percentage of startups get funded, either through sheer persistence or a stroke of luck.

Once this first round of capital is raised, a new set of challenges arises. Investors, driven by the desire for a substantial financial return, seek milestones, demonstrable progress, new rounds of financing at higher prices, or even quick exits. While some investors may be patient, taking a decade or longer view to helping build the company, others are more anxious to see quick progress. In many cases, these investors view the company as partly their own, which it in fact is, now that they've invested in it. Some of these investors are happy to support the entrepreneur in any way the entrepreneur needs them to. Other investors have their own view of what they, and the entrepreneur, should be doing—providing oversight, and "adding value" to the startup through their role on the board.

A long-standing cliché in the venture capital world is that VCs provide "adult supervision" to the entrepreneurs. We find this language to be pejorative and insulting to the entrepreneur and the company, so we try to avoid it. Instead of talking in abstractions, we'll describe clearly what VCs and board members can do to be helpful to the companies whose boards they serve on. We'll be equally direct about describing what entrepreneurs and management can do to engage these directors.

A board of directors can be created at the inception of the company and is almost always formed in conjunction with the first outside financing. Many early-stage companies never convene a board on a regular basis. In bootstrapped companies, the entrepreneurs have no outside investors so they often feel no need to create a board since they feel responsible only to themselves.

In all cases we think this is a mistake and believe you should form your board early in the life of your company, regardless of how you are financed. If you do it correctly, choose the right directors, and engage them actively, they can help you dramatically accelerate your business. Then when you run into trouble, they can help guide you through the tough spots.

Clint Korver (Ulu Ventures, Partner) teaches a course on startup boards at Stanford University called "Startup Boards: Advanced Entrepreneurship." Clint says, "The most common mistake startups make is *not* having a board at all." He points out that research shows a majority of startups fail due to self-inflicted wounds—internal decisions about founding team, roles, equity, and other important issues. "Founders who are overconfident or choose to avoid conflict often miss an opportunity to bring in fresh perspective and structure these decisions from appropriate individuals," says Clint. "The other common mistake founders make is to populate the board with friends and family—you need to think carefully if they can address challenges or make decisions in the interest of the startup. Finally, often only founders populate the startups board—this often leads to confusion with respect to decision making and authority."

THE BOARD IS AN EXTENSION OF YOUR TEAM

The search for capital can be agonizing. When a term sheet is on the horizon, most founders are ecstatic that the long process of raising the venture round is almost over. During this process, many founders ignore the type of board members that come with the money. Smart founders understand that building a great company is all about the people and the members of the board are just as important as the early employees. "If I was prepping my younger brother on a startup journey, I would tell him to raise money only from those investors who can strategically add value and emotionally connect with you to help you be better," says Foundry Group managing director Jason Mendelson.

Once you've taken investment from VCs, they will ensure their investment has some protection as a result of control provisions in the financing document. They'll also have a governance role as a result of their board seat. But more importantly they become part of the company as a result of their role on the board. While founders and investors often fret over control issues, Union Square Ventures partner Fred Wilson points out, "Boards should not be controlled by the founder, the CEO, or the largest shareholder. For a board to do its job, it must represent all stakeholders' interests, not just one stakeholder's interest."[2]

The best entrepreneurs construct a board of directors the same way they build their core management team, recruiting the best people they can find for the roles that are needed. A great board member can be a superb coach and mentor—pushing you to grow, encouraging you to take on bigger challenges, and ultimately reaching your highest potential. Like any great coach, he will be careful never to undermine you or jump in the driver's seat.

Not all board members understand this. Some feel the need to manage the CEO and the entrepreneurs. Others can't help but get involved in minutiae stir up conflict, and try to solve problems that they see emerging. This type of board member behavior gets in the way of the functioning of the company, confuses the management team, and, in the worst cases, damages the startup.

Constructing a good board starts with identifying investors and board members who understand the world of startups, know the dynamics of your market, and bring unique positive attributes that are often much more important than money. Founders, especially early in the life of a company, often feel like they have to make trade-offs to take money when it's available, rather than patiently seeking the right investor for their startup. Being patient is worth it—ultimately having the right personalities will help make the journey of a startup CEO easier.

Boards can significantly impact the trajectory of a startup. A great board is a mix of intellect, experience, personalities, ego, emotions, and aspirations that, when combined correctly, can be a strong net positive experience for the company. It can be magical when a diverse set of experiences among board members—including product development, business strategy, financial expertise, general management skills, and broad network reach—are joined effectively. In contrast, when the ingredients don't mix well, it can be a disaster.

Your board is your inner sanctum and your strategic planning department.[3] The board guides, engages regularly, and builds a deep relationship with the CEO. But it is not simply a friendship—the board expects results and accountability. Value creation is a cliché in a startup's vocabulary, but if a CEO ignores the goal of building a valuable business, boards, especially those loaded with investors, will often turn against a CEO.

In this book, we'll talk about how to construct the board, lead and manage it, and deal with conflicts when they arise. We'll also help you understand how to get the most out of your board and how to address things when they aren't working. While a great board can be a guidepost and a positive catalyst, a bad board can cause angst and frustration, destroy value, and occasionally kill a company. Don't ever forget the cliché "success results from the entrepreneur, failure belongs to the board."

WHO THIS BOOK IS FOR

Our goal with the books in the Startup Revolution series (http://startuprev .com) is to help any entrepreneur, regardless of experience, location, or type of company. While we've written this book with the first-time entrepreneur in mind, we believe each book in the series applies to entrepreneurs with any level of experience. Having a "beginner's mind" often helps you learn new things. If you are an experienced entrepreneur, we hope this is one of those cases.

We've also written this book for board members. Over the past 20 years, we've encountered and worked with thousands of board members covering a wide range of experiences. While a few of these board members were spectacular and had a dramatic, positive impact on the trajectory and outcome of the company, many were average and had a neutral or insignificant impact. Others were detrimental. We've learned a lot from all of these experiences—both good and bad—and have tried to incorporate this learning into this book in a way that is helpful to any board member regardless of experience.

This book is also for management teams. Most management teams are directly exposed to the board and interact with them on a regular basis. This can be extremely helpful or completely disruptive. The responsibility of a successful relationship between board members and members of the management team belongs to both the board members and the management team. As a result, we think every executive in a startup company can benefit from this book.

Throughout this book we've incorporated the advice of many investors, board members, entrepreneurs, and executives whose views we respect. We've used stories and examples that emphasize certain points. We give plenty of advice and provide tools for implementing this advice. However, we are still learning, so we'll continue to write about our experience, new experiments, and things we learn on the Startup Revolution web site at http://startuprev.com.

MAGIC WORDS, PHRASES, AND ABBREVIATIONS

Having written several books, we've come to learn how important it is to be precise with certain words and phrases. This book was particularly tricky given the different roles participants play in a board, so we'll define a few right now. Our goal, as with everything we do, is inclusiveness, so you should err on the side of a broader definition when you encounter a magic word, unless we specify otherwise.

> *Entrepreneur* and *founder:* We use these two words interchangeably. To us, they mean the same thing.
>
> *CEO:* The CEO can be one of the founders, but doesn't have to be. Occasionally, we'll refer to "founder/CEO" when this is an important distinction.
>
> *Angel investor:* We include "friends and family" and "seed" investors in the definition of an "angel investor." So when you see "angel investor," you know we are talking about the early investors in a company who are investing their own money. We do not ever include "seed VCs" in this category, although the angel investors could be the seed investors.

VC: We often abbreviate "venture capitalist" as "VC." It takes the word count down significantly and is a lot more readable.

Board: We'll start abbreviating "board of directors" as "board." There's that word count thing again.

Chair: While "chairman of the board" sounds serious and weighty, there are plenty of "chairwomen." We prefer to use "chair" since it's gender neutral.

We've written this book together. While we each have a different set of experiences, we felt it would be more effective to use one voice. We'll often refer to one of us in the third person; if you've read the book *Startup Life: Surviving and Thriving with an Entrepreneur* that Brad wrote with his wife, Amy Batchelor, you are already used to this approach.

Okay, let's get started.

CHAPTER TWO

WHAT IS A BOARD?

C ooley LLP partner Eric Jensen, who represents companies like LinkedIn and Adobe, describes corporate governance as "processes, customs, policies, and laws affecting the way a corporation is directed, administered, and controlled." He goes on to say, "While local state laws are important, the right processes and policies are of equal or greater importance. Many companies just get going and assume that the right practices will develop."

A board of directors has a set of formal duties, which are often referred to as *corporate governance*. They include legal concepts such as *duty of care* and *duty of loyalty* as well as committees such as the audit, compensation, and nominating committees. While startup boards should be nimble, it is useful to understand the formal requirements.

As a startup grows, the number of stakeholders increases. At the time of its inception, a startup may have a small team, often just the founders. A few early employees are added and given stock options. A seed round is completed, which adds a few angel investors. The company releases its product; customers and suppliers become stakeholders in the startup. More employees are added, and a venture capital round is completed. Soon, you have a number of differing interests, some short term and some long term, related to the company. At times, these interests conflict with each other. The board ultimately is responsible for navigating any conflicts that arise.

Rather than defaulting into whatever processes start to happen, excellent founders focus early on putting a structure in place to ensure that the board develops governance policies and procedures to minimize conflicts of interest and maximize shareholder value. Good boards invite counsel to participate in meetings to ensure that best practices are being followed. While entrepreneurs are rightfully concerned about racking up legal fees in such situations, Eric Jensen states, "Just as a VC is focused on building the company using best practices, a good attorney does not focus just on legal aspects. We act as advisers first; we sit in such board meetings for free and alert the CEO to any warning signs we spot in these board meetings."

Developing a *code of conduct* that establishes the ground rules of behavior, especially under conflicting circumstances, is helpful at this stage. More often than not, short-term challenges trounce the need for preparing such a code. However, when you do take the effort to prepare such a document, it establishes the ground rules and can be incredibly helpful, especially when conflicts arise.[1]

VALUE CREATION, ACCOUNTABILITY, AND TRANSPARENCY

One of the primary roles of a board is to ensure that the interests of all the shareholders are being considered. In many startups, the primary shareholders and board members are often the same, consisting of the founders, CEO, and investors. As companies grow and develop, outside board members, who aren't involved in the business and don't have a significant economic stake, get added. Collectively, this group is responsible for considering and balancing the interests of all the shareholders.

In addition to working to maximize the value of an economic outcome, the board also ensures accountability and transparency. In a formal sense, the CEO presents the ongoing progress of a company and gives a periodic account of the business operations to the board. It is then the board's responsibility to establish appropriate procedures, set milestones, and assess performance. Transparency ensures that all actions of the CEO and the board are conducted based on factual information with sound judgment and the interests of all shareholders in mind.

Functionally, the CEO works for the board. Graphicly CEO Micah Baldwin states, "As soon as you raise money, it's no longer your company—you are now working for somebody else. If you don't perform, you will get fired. If I don't get fired, then I know I've had a good board meeting. This reminds me every month of my responsibilities."

As a board member, a venture capitalist (VC) needs to act in the interest of the company, representing all shareholders, rather than their narrow interest as an investor. This is often a difficult conflict for an investor to manage, and you'll often hear VCs qualifying their statements in a board context using phrases such as "I'm wearing my investor hat now." But as August

Capital partner Andy Rappaport says, "I have a test I use. Can I explain my decision as reasonable and fair to any shareholder group, not just my own?"

LEGAL DUTIES OF A BOARD MEMBER

The state laws in which the company is incorporated along with the company's charter documents (the articles of incorporation, bylaws, and shareholder rights) establish the legal duties of a board member. For public companies, the Securities and Exchange Commission (SEC) adds some bonus rules.

A fiduciary duty is an obligation of a board member to act in the best interest of another party. Every board member has a fiduciary duty to the shareholders. A fiduciary duty is the highest standard of care, and a fiduciary is expected to be extremely loyal to the person or entity to whom she owes the duty (the "principal"): she must not put her personal interests before the duty and must not profit from her position as a fiduciary, unless the principal consents.

About 10 years ago, I was in a board meeting when management told the board that they had uncovered significant accounting issues in a recently acquired company. This was a public company board. And these accounting issues had flowed through to several quarterly financial statements that had been reported to the public. Every board member who was also a material shareholder (me included) knew that the minute this information was disclosed, our shareholdings would plummet in value. But there was no question what we had to do. We had to hire a law firm to investigate the accounting issues. We had to immediately disclose the findings to the public. And we had to terminate all the employees who had any involvement in this matter. Things like fiduciary responsibility seem very theoretical until you find yourself in a moment like this. Then they become crystal clear.

Fred Wilson, Partner, Union Square Ventures,
www.avc.com/a_vc/2012/03/the-board-of-directors-role-and-responsibilities.html

Board members are bound by two formal legal obligations: the *duty of care* and the *duty of loyalty*. These are defined as follows:

Duty of care: A board member is to conduct all actions in a manner where they see no foreseeable harm. A board member needs to be attentive and prudent in making board-level decisions, act in good faith, and conduct sufficient investigations to provide a logical basis for decisions. A board member breaches his duty of care when he acts in a negligent manner or knows that the consequences of an action could be harmful to the company.

Duty of loyalty: A board member should ensure that interests of the company are always first and foremost in his mind and that loyalty to the company supersedes any other vested interests he might have. Duty of loyalty is breached when a board member puts his personal interest ahead of the company, conducts inappropriate transactions that benefit the board member (known as *self-dealing*), or benefits personally from confidential information shared in the boardroom.

Since investor board members are also trying to make a financial return, conflicts of interest can arise at every step. As True Ventures managing partner Jon Callaghan puts it, "As long as you are a board member, you have to focus on what is best for all shareholders. This can be difficult for VCs. Afterwards, you can go home and fret all you want about your fund not making a better return."

There are additional duties referred to as the *duty of confidentiality* and the *duty of disclosure*. While these are linked to the duty of care and duty of loyalty, they are just as important. They are defined as follows:

Duty of confidentiality: A subset of the duty of loyalty, this requires a director to maintain the confidentiality of nonpublic information about the company.

Duty of disclosure: A director, pursuant to the duties of care and loyalty, is required to take reasonable steps to ensure that a company provides its stockholders with all material information relating to a matter for which stockholder action is sought.

While these duties may sound good conceptually, in practice they are subject to judgment and interpretation based on the specific situation. A legal construct, referred to as the *business judgment rule*, governs the specific interpretation. The business judgment rule is used to test whether the director acts in good faith, in an informed manner, while putting his personal interests below those of the corporation. Specifically, the director is following the business judgment rule if he:

- Does not have any personal interest in the outcome.
- Has reviewed all information prior to making a decision.
- Believes that the decision is in the best interests of the company.

This rule helps protect a director from personal liability for allegedly bad business decisions by essentially shifting the burden of proof to a plaintiff to demonstrate that the director did not satisfy his fiduciary duties.

CHAIR OR LEAD DIRECTOR

Boards need a leader. Historically, this role has been titled "chairman," although we prefer to shorten it simply to "chair." More recently, as the debate over the split between chair and CEO has intensified, a new construct—that of a "lead director"—has emerged. For most purposes, *chairman, chair*, and *lead director* are interchangeable.

While in many cases a founder or the CEO is also the chair of the board, there are plenty of situations where you want a board chair separate from the CEO or founder. For some investors, this is a requirement.

If your lead investor has experience as a board chair, that's often a good solution. However, many VC investors have no experience as a board chair, lack an understanding of the role of a board chair, or have a history of overplaying their role as board chair. Be wary of this and do your diligence into the VC as a potential board chair, just like you would with any other board member.

A board chair's role differs from that of any board member—not all board members can be good board chairs. This role calls for subtle skills above and beyond what any board member may bring to the table. Following are some specific characteristics of a good board chair:

Ensures alignment. The board exists to help the company be successful. But definitions of success vary. A good chair keeps an eye on the big picture and ensures each meeting is a step in the right direction. When a board member gets off track, or worse, tries to derail meetings, has a specific agenda, or causes other random disruptions, the board chair will need to take action.

Is decisive. The board meeting is a place where information is shared and decisions are made. People want to be heard. Loud voices can often drown out quieter voices. This dynamic can occasionally get out of hand. Some board members focus on showing how smart they are, while others lock horns around seemingly trivial issues. A good board chair allows all voices to be heard, draws out the quieter participants, and gets all the relevant information out on the table while simultaneously driving the discussion to a decision in a timely manner.

Is a proactive communicator. A good board chair manages all one-on-one communications proactively with the CEO. While any board member can choose to mentor and guide the CEO, the board chair has a special responsibility for synthesizing all of the feedback and delivering it to the CEO in a consistent manner.

Manages the clock. Board members are busy people with significant and conflicting demands on their time. Beginning and ending the meeting on time, conforming to a predefined agenda, and moving the conversation along when it stalls is critical.

Maintains culture and hygiene. As an advocate of the company, the board chair creates and maintains a positive and constructive culture, especially in times of challenge and stress. Wasting time, allowing a hostile dynamic between board members to become the norm, alienating individual board members, or overemphasizing individual flaws is not helpful.

An effective lead director (or independent chair) can help facilitate a thoughtful, fair, and balanced discussion of strategy, team, and execution issues. Successful boards achieve an appropriate balance between management and board perspectives and a full and fair discussion of key issues and challenges facing the company. This dynamic can improve management team thinking while better informing the board members about the company issues and strategy.

Lead directors can play a role in ensuring there is balance in the boardroom and all important constituencies and perspectives are represented, and can help ensure noncore agendas or perspectives do not obscure discussions.

Startups generally succeed and become great companies because they have capable teams focused on attractive markets. This is often coupled with a healthy paranoia about what can and is going wrong. So how do boards help with this?

Good boards help companies clarify and sharpen management team thinking, triage risks and priorities, and provide perspectives based on experienced wisdom or insight that informs judgment. Successful boards understand that they are not running the company but are best able to provide perspective not clouded by having to fight the day-to-day battles.

There are two common failure modes for early-stage boards. The first one happens when directors believe they are best positioned to direct short-term operational detail. This can result in confusion about company leadership among the management team and disempowers the CEO. More important, it does not allow the CEO to grow and develop.

In this scenario, current or former operating executives who may lack sufficient situational awareness or excessively apply their historical patterns or insights to their board role sometimes populate boards. When this happens, a lead director can be effective in helping the CEO and team tease out the relevant observations and structure the insights as advice rather than prescriptive direction.

Overly prescriptive board members often cause great frustration for the CEO. While they value the experience and insight, the CEO might also believe the director lacks context or market relevance. It is a tall order for a young CEO to push back and reframe the discussion. Lead directors should be active in coaching the CEO and director to get topics on the table for consideration in a constructive context.

The second common failure mode for young company boards can be focusing the company and board discussion on noncore issues. Startups often have venture partners or associates as board members. Some of the best board members are venture capitalists; they can have great pattern matching, market insight, and networks that many operating executives envy. Some, however, suffer from a lack of operating experience and perspective, particularly early in careers before analytical skills are more developed. There can be a tendency to direct the company to the latest trend or perhaps a strategy that has been successful at another company that may not have full relevance to the current company. Board time is a scarce resource and should not be wasted. Correction of this boardroom dynamic is complicated by the fact that these board members are entitled to their seat and perspective by their investment in the company.

Whether it is a VC or independent board member, the tendency to focus on non-core issues is often driven by a desire to contribute and add value. There are two strategies that can be effective in dealing with this challenge. In the board meeting, the CEO or lead director can steer the meeting back to the core topics. In the long run, one-on-one conversations between the lead director and all other directors are very effective in allowing each board member to be heard while getting consensus on the most important issues for the company.

People often ask, "What makes boards effective?" The best CEOs generally believe they get great insight, balance, and perspective from their board. They often characterize themselves as myopic—overly focused on internal issues or paranoid about what they don't know. Boards help them see a broader horizon, apply judgment to issues and risks, and can help teams frame and prioritize.

Effective boards tend to be characterized by a constructive culture where there is mutual respect among the board and team members, honesty where candid discussion of issues and challenges naturally happens, and a diverse set of skills and backgrounds that help ensure full consideration of topics.

Lead directors play a unique role in helping CEOs build and operate effective boards. It starts with recruiting effective independent board members. Focus should be given to background and skills fit, but especially to cultural fit. Is this person someone the CEO and other board members will respect and trust? Will he bring experience or perspectives we need but don't currently have? If times get tough (and they likely will at some point), is this someone we can count on to bring good judgment to a hard set of problems?

Boards should have dialog with the CEO without the management team members and among themselves without the CEO. In the latter discussion, the lead director should facilitate the conversation, ensuring that all perspectives are heard and fairly represented but framed in the right context. It is natural to give equal weight to all comments. However, all insights are not equal. The lead director should balance insights with judgment to ensure that the feedback to the CEO reflects the proper prioritization.

Finally, the lead director should play an active role in board governance, helping ensure that the board has an effective means to calibrate its performance as a team as well as assess the contributions of various board members. This should include assessments of the board committees and their effectiveness. It is also important to review the performance of the lead director by other board members. This can be done in a group discussion (without the lead director) or in a formal assessment. In all cases, boards and lead directors will benefit from a candid discussion of how they can improve.

The lead director plays a unique role among board members. The most effective lead directors can help the CEO organize the agenda and board discussion to focus on the most important topics, facilitate discussions among the board, and help ensure that the board operates in a culture of openness and honesty.

Tom Bogan, Greylock Partner, Citrix and Rally Software Lead Director

THE ROLE OF BOARD COMMITTEES

Early in the life of a company, the board is often small, numbering between three and five members. At this point in the company's development, board business is often presented simultaneously to the entire board. As Orbotix

CEO Paul Berberian correctly points out, "In startup boards, there is not much to govern—the board has to support the CEO with their resources, opinions, and their experience—where they see what has worked in other companies and what has not."

However, as a company grows, its board of directors, and the amount of things the board needs to consider, grows as well. As the level of oversight of the board increases, specific committees, including audit, compensation, and nominating, are often formed. Existing board members serve on these committees, with board members often serving on multiple committees. The charter of a company, and of the specific committees, will reflect the formation of such committees and how each committee carries out its responsibilities, including structure, processes, and membership requirements.

The specific definition and responsibilities of the audit, compensation, and nominating committees follows:

> *Audit committee:* Oversees the company's accounting and financial reporting processes and financial audits. The responsibilities include ensuring timely audits, independence of audits, and communicating with the independent auditors about any relationships or services that could affect the auditor's objectivity and independence.
>
> *Compensation committee:* Establishes CEO and executive officer compensation, oversees equity compensation grant policy, and hires outside experts to provide opinions as needed on market-based compensation ranges.
>
> *Nominating committee:* Recruit and orient new directors, manage CEO succession planning, and monitor governance processes.

OTHER FUNCTIONS OF A BOARD

While we have been discussing formal responsibilities of the board, often the informal ones are just as important. Following are several of the most important informal functions of a board:

> *Ensuring survival.* One of the most important tasks of a board member is ensuring that the startup stays alive. Startups can run out of cash, face schisms between the founders, or get sued out of existence by patent trolls. In a December 2011 presentation made at Angel

Capital Association, Ohio TechAngels founder Richard Huston points out that the board's main task is to make sure a company never runs out of cash. While no one can guarantee survival, stepping up to help when a company is in distress is a fundamental role of a board member.

Establishing financial controls. A board establishes procedures and policies to establish financial controls. These typically include (a) two signatories, such as the CEO and CFO, on most checks; and (b) board approvals for major expenses, which may be defined as an amount, for example, any expenditures above $100,000. From an entrepreneur's perspective, if the board approves an annual operating budget, such controls are easier to handle if any significant deviations occur, as the board can approve those as opposed to the CEO seeking approval for every item. As the company matures, audits of financial statements become the norm, governed by the audit committee. While this process requires considerable time and effort on the part of management, it ensures appropriate accounting practices are followed.

Developing reporting guidelines. The board should aim to help the shareholders understand the status of the business in a timely manner. Often, a term sheet will include formal reporting requirements. Example language from the term sheet is:

The Company will deliver to such Major Investor (i) annual, quarterly, and monthly financial statements, and other information as determined by the Board; (ii) thirty days prior to the end of each fiscal year, a comprehensive operating budget forecasting the Company's revenues, expenses, and cash position on a month-to-month basis for the upcoming fiscal year; and (iii) promptly following the end of each quarter an up-to-date capitalization table.

Regardless of whether the formal reporting requirements are defined, the actual reporting is the responsibility of the CEO. A good board will encourage a CEO to send these reports out in a timely manner.

Conducting CEO performance assessment and conflict resolution. While many companies have an internal review process, this is often overlooked for the CEO. The board can provide the framework for this and result in a robust CEO review on an annual basis. In addition, when conflicts between the CEO and co-founders, or other members of the management team arise, the board often plays the role of conflict resolver. For example, an entrepreneur we work with recently stated, "My co-founder and I were having a lot of conflict on various day-to-day issues. Our VC pulled me aside and said, 'We have one CEO—that's you. You need to put your partner in a box. If you can't do it, you shouldn't be the CEO.' I had to finally learn how to manage my co-founder. We got through it successfully, had a good outcome, and remained friends, but it was tough."

There are many other informal functions of a board and the individual board members. We'll go into them much deeper in later chapters.

PART TWO

BUILDING YOUR BOARD

CHAPTER THREE

CREATING YOUR BOARD

The startup journey can be a lonely one for the CEO. It's filled with ups and downs, unexpected stresses, and an endless number of decisions. Surrounding yourself with the best minds both on your team and on your board is an important part of this journey. Often, entrepreneurs raise money from investors without considering the competence or fit of these investors and end up with investors who may be arrogant, ignorant, or incompetent. This can be toxic to the company and destructive to the psyche of the CEO and the founders.

As difficult as it may be, great entrepreneurs seek the right balance of character and capital from investors. You can compromise on the latter but never on the former. The art of proactively building your board, even as you seek to engage the best-in-class investors and integrate their capital and minds with your startup, will benefit you greatly in the long-term. While investors bring capital to the table, great board members bring capital, experience, and an emotional foundation to help the startup, the entrepreneurs, and the CEO succeed through the inevitable ups and downs of creating a company.

THE BOARD'S TECHNICAL PRIORITIES: ECONOMICS AND CONTROL

As explained in *Venture Deals: Be Smarter Than Your Lawyer and Venture Capitalist*, the two primary characteristics of every investment are economics and control. While economics are often well defined, control is subtler, as the terms regarding control may be decoupled from the actual economics and buried in the nuance of the financing documents.

In any startup, there can be multiple layers of control. The first interplay is between the CEO and the board. The CEO controls the day-to-day business and operating decisions of the company and allocation of resources to achieve the plan. The CEO sets the annual plan, but the board approves it. The CEO hires and recommends compensation for the next layer of management; the board approves it. However, the board can fire and replace the CEO.

The founders and noninvestor shareholders have various controls based on the number of shares outstanding, specific voting rights, and corporate law. However, this level of control can be elusive after a financing, especially in the context of the *protective provisions* of the investors. The protective provisions can include changing the terms of stock owned by the investors, authorizing the creation of more stock, issuing any stock senior or equal to the investors, buying back any of the common stock, selling the company, changing the certificate of incorporation or bylaw, changing the size of the board of directors, declaring or paying a dividend, and borrowing money. Investors can also have drag-along rights, which compel other shareholders to vote with them in certain situations, as well as conversion rights, which give them control over when they convert their preferred stock into common stock.

Additionally, the board members will have *fiduciary duties to all shareholders* independent of their status as shareholders. This often creates intellectual dissonance for some investor board members, as they struggle to determine whether they are playing a board member role or an investor role in certain contexts.

Noam Wasserman (Harvard Business School professor and author of *The Founders Dilemma*) states the conflict between economics and control clearly. "If you don't figure out which matters more to you, you could end up being neither rich nor king." While some entrepreneurs end up accomplishing being rich and king, this is the exception, not the rule. Wasserman's advice is to the point: if you care more about control, seriously consider not raising any capital. Instead, bootstrap your company. Also, never forget that startups have a high failure rate; many vanish into oblivion where neither fame nor fortune is achieved.

The document that describes your rights as an owner or shareholder is the *shareholder rights agreement*. All shareholders enjoy some rights, which are governed by the *articles of incorporation* of the company and the laws of the state in which the company is incorporated. These rights can include:

- *Voting rights, including right to elect the directors.* The directors represent the interests of shareholders.

- *Inspection of corporate books and records.* This allows shareholders to review the decision-making process of the board as well as the financial records of the company. In some states, such as California, minority shareholders have the right to inspect two different sets of records: (1) record of shareholders; and (2) accounting books, records, and minutes of proceedings. These rights cannot be modified by the startup's bylaws.
- *Initiating actions against directors for illegal or fraudulent activities.* For example, California law states that shareholders can exercise their rights in these conditions:[1]
  - Removal of directors for cause or by court proceedings.
  - A director's standard of care.
  - Officers' and directors' indemnification.
  - The liability of directors and shareholders for unlawful distributions.
  - Dissenters' rights.

In contrast to the control provisions, which are tightly defined in advance, economic performance is tied to the progress of a startup. The CEO and the executives, through their day-to-day actions, drive the economic outcomes of a company. As the company progresses along product and revenue milestones, the cash position, revenues, profits, and ultimately valuation is impacted. Consider the following examples:

- If a CEO and the team are unable to meet product development, revenue, or other commercial milestones, the value of the company, and thus the shareholders financial outcomes, will deteriorate.
- If the company makes great progress on milestones but runs out of cash, new or existing investors may propose additional financing at a lower valuation, commonly referred to as a *down round.* When a board approves a financing at a down round, all of the current shareholders will be impacted.

While the ultimate decision of a board is hiring and firing the CEO, the board also has a number of other responsibilities that impact the economics of the company, including approving:

- The annual budget and operating plan.
- Compensation plans and stock option grants.
- Any financing, debt, and expenses above a certain threshold.
- Creation of a new class of shares or expansion of an option pool.

The span of control of the CEO differs from company to company, although in most startups, this can overlap with the board to a large extent, especially since the CEO is almost always also a member of the board. Table 3.1 delineates some of the key responsibilities between your board and the CEO.

TABLE 3.1 Key Responsibilities of the CEO and the Board

	CEO	Both CEO and Board	Board Members
Overall goals	Sets the overall vision and strategy of the company and communicates it to all stakeholders. Recruits, hires, and retains the very best talent for the company. Makes sure there is always enough cash in the bank.	Ensure alignment, accountability, and transparency.	Economics, governance, and control. Develop policies and procedures to support the CEO and the company.
Team	Recruits, hires, evaluates, and fires team members.	Develop annual hiring and stock option plan.	Hire and fire the CEO. Evaluate CEO performance. Evaluate board performance.
Budget and Plan	Develops annual budget and plan for board approval.	Review and modify budget and plan.	Approve annual budget and plan.
Execution	Executes on plan and suggests corrective action.	Modify plan based on market conditions.	Monitor performance of the company.
Operations	Product development, sales, and marketing.	Ensure policies and processes are established.	Confirm and review tax, audit, and regulatory compliance.
Financial	Maintains records and accounts, and produces monthly statements.	Review performance. Capital structure planning.	Assist with financing and review audit.

From Fred Wilson's spectacular post on "What a CEO Does" at www.avc.com/a_vc/2010/08/what-a-ceo-does.html

THE BOARD'S EMOTIONAL PRIORITIES: TRUST, JUDGMENT, AND TRANSPARENCY

While the technical priorities of the board tend to be concrete, well defined, and legally constructed, the emotional priorities are the opposite: soft, qualitative, fluid, and dependent on personalities.

Trust among board members is by far the most critical of these emotional priorities. In the absence of trust, you simply will not have an effective board. Trust is hard to earn and easy to lose. While board members will have different personalities and may have divergent goals and polarizing or conflicting styles, an underlying basis of trust among all board members is foundational to the success of the board as well as the company. If this trust is broken, in any way, the first priority of the board should be to reestablish it.

While trust tends to be binary—it either exists or it doesn't—judgment tends to be issue specific. Board members will have various levels of experience with different issues and their ability to make sound judgments varies based on this experience and the information they are presented with. Self-awareness is key—a board member who is aware that he is not an expert on a particular issue, or who explicitly qualifies his confidence in his opinion on a specific matter, is a much more valuable board member than one who "knows everything" and strongly asserts a statement of fact on any issue.

The notion of transparency creates glue between trust and judgment. To be transparent, all issues and opinions should be discussed openly. Any conflict, especially between board members, should be brought up to the entire board to discuss. While there will be one-off discussions between board members, or closed sessions where management is not included in the discussion, ultimately all issues discussed should be surfaced to all board members. This transparency will enable a board to function effectively through any circumstance—good or bad.

COMPOSITION OF THE BOARD

The composition of the board, including the skills and experience of each board member, is important to think through carefully, and will vary based

TABLE 3.2 The Role of Board Members at Different Stages of a Company

	Startup	Revenue	Growth
Role of Board Member/ Company Needs	Working/Active	Shaping/Nurturing	Governing/ Monitoring
Customer Discovery and Market Development	High	Moderate	Low
Product Development	High	Moderate/High	Low
Sales and Marketing	High/Moderate	High	High
Finance and Operational Controls	Moderate/Low	Moderate	High
Human Resources	Low	Moderate	High
Strategy	High	High	High

on the stage of the company. Table 3.2 is a useful framework for the different skills needed at different stages of a company.

While a person who has great finance, audit, regulatory, and cost control expertise would be a suitable board member for a growth company preparing for an initial public offering (IPO), he is likely less effective for a startup of three people that is pre-product and pre-revenue.

One of the guys who taught me the venture capital business used to say "success is in inverse proportion to the number of VCs you have on your board." The best question asked of management in a board meeting was asked by an independent director who happens to be a CEO of a company that is five times bigger than our portfolio company. In the midst of "celebratory" talk, he brought everyone back to reality and got folks to think about what we could be doing better. It was a great board moment. The CEO was seeking advice on some important strategic questions. And this five-member board had four very experienced operating executives giving the CEO advice. It was a great meeting. I walked out thinking that is the way a board should be constructed. A perfect board would include the CEO of the startup, an investor, and three other CEOs who have built and/or run one or more tech companies of scale. If you have a very experienced VC on your board, you really don't need more of them. But you can never have enough peers on your board who have been where you are before. That is invaluable.

Fred Wilson, Partner, Union Square Ventures,
www.avc.com/a_vc/2013/01/who-you-want-on-your-board.html

At the early stages of a company the founders should lead the board formation process. As a company evolves, the responsibility for the configuration and evolution of the board often shifts to the CEO and the largest investors. As the company continues to grow and the board interactions become more formalized, a *nominating committee* consisting of several board members, who could include the CEO and founders, gets created. In each of these cases, all board members should actively contribute to defining the composition of the board.

IDENTIFYING GREAT BOARD MEMBERS

Entrepreneurs put tremendous energy into recruiting a phenomenal vice president of engineering, hiring the best developers, and building an amazing sales organization. But when it comes to attracting board members, many entrepreneurs are casual, or even passive, about recruiting great board members.

While a venture capitalist (VC) board member is often a requirement of an investment, you generally also have the option of adding one or more outside board members early in the life of your startup and over time transitioning your board more heavily toward noninvestor board members. As an entrepreneur, it's your responsibility to do your homework and understand the character of any potential board member, even if they are a prospective investor. A common cliché is that investors buy their board seat—in most cases, once you have them on the board, it's difficult to get rid of them.

A great board member has, at the minimum, the following attributes:

- *Bold mindset.* A board member at an early stage company understands the startup trajectory, which is often a roller coaster ride without the barf bags. The board member is comfortable with ambiguity, can make decisions with imperfect information, and has a bias for taking action. He can be brutally honest, calling out weaknesses and problems he sees, while delivering feedback in a calm and constructive fashion. While he is articulate, he doesn't serve up banal platitudes, blather on like a perpetual Pollyanna, or endlessly ask questions. He is balanced emotionally and, as Union Square Ventures partner Fred Wilson says, has "great judgment and ethics."[2]
- *Entrepreneurial experience.* Experience as a founder, CEO, or executive in an entrepreneurial company is highly desirable for early-stage

company board members. While there is an endless argument about whether VCs who were once entrepreneurs are better than VCs who were never entrepreneurs, VCs who have never been entrepreneurs can have extraordinary amounts of entrepreneurial experience based on the companies they've been investors in. Steve Blank (serial entrepreneur and author of *The Startup Owners Manual* and *The Four Steps to the Epiphany*) writes, "A veteran board can bring 50–100× more experience into a board meeting than a first time founder. VCs sit on 6–12 boards at a time. Assume an average tenure of 4 years per board. Assume two veteran VCs per board = 50–100× more experience."[3]

- *Domain expertise.* A strong network and connections within the industry or market you are operating in can be a big advantage. "If I was picking a VC, I would pick one based on similar investments they've made. The greatest value we've gotten is from companies that are in the same sector and would help us propel ours. VCs have leverage over their portfolio and can accelerate partnerships," says VictorOps CEO Todd Vernon. Niel Robertson, CEO of Trada, who has served on a half-dozen VC-backed company boards, adds, "I have studiously avoided MBA-type board members who learn how to run a business by attending board meetings at the expense of the startup. I just think it is obnoxious. I've not let such people invest in my company—they would not be a good fit as a board member."

While a CEO may look for different functional attributes in each board member, the general characteristics are often the same. Return Path CEO Matt Blumberg succinctly describes what he looks for as follows:

They are prepared and keep commitments. They show up to all meetings. They show up on time and don't leave early. They do their homework. They are fully present and don't do e-mail during meetings.

They speak their minds. They have no fear of bringing up an uncomfortable topic during a meeting, even if it impacts someone in the room. They do not come up to you after a meeting and tell you what they really think. I had a board member once tell my entire management team that he thought I needed to be better at firing executives more quickly!

They build independent relationships. They get to know each other and see each other outside of your meetings. They get to know individuals on your management team and talk to them on occasion as well. None of this communication goes through you.

They are resource rich. I've had some directors who are one-trick or two-trick ponies with their advice. After their third or fourth meeting, they have nothing new to add. Board members should be able to pull from years of experience and adapt that experience to your situations on a flexible and dynamic basis.

They are strategically engaged but operationally distant. This may vary by stage of company and the needs of your own team, but I find that even board members who are talented operators have a hard time parachuting into any given situation and being super useful. Getting their operational help requires a lot of regular engagement on a specific issue or area. But they must be strategically engaged and understand the fundamental dynamics and drivers of your business—economics, competition, ecosystem, and the like.

Matt Blumberg, CEO, Return Path,
www.onlyonceblog.com/2012/02/what-makes-an-awesome-board-member

THE VC FIRM MATTERS AS MUCH AS THE PERSON

VCs typically conduct a significant amount of due diligence on the founders, the CEO, and the management team before they invest in a company. Entrepreneurs should do the same with prospective investors and board members. In assessing fit, entrepreneurs should not only look at individual attributes but also understand how group dynamics may alter an individual's behavior. The composition of the board and the interplay between different board members is the first step in assessing prospective board members.

While individual attributes are important, a great board member who is part of a less-than-stellar VC firm is like a great singer in a lousy band— neither benefit from each other, undermining what can be good about each of them. As you evaluate the VCs you are talking to, pay attention to the following three areas as you explore their firm:

- *Capital.* Does the VC firm's current fund have the ability to invest across multiple rounds of your company? If it's not clear, ask directly to understand how they approach financings, how they reserve for follow-on financings, and whether they require a new investor to lead subsequent rounds. Also, ask how much capital they have available in their fund for future investments.

- *Firm stability.* How long have the partners in the firm worked together? Is the partner you are talking to new to the firm, or has he been there for many years? Has there been recent turnover or changes in the partners at the firm? Ask other entrepreneurs what their perception of the firm is—don't rely on articles in the tech press.
- *Strong portfolio with demonstrated exits.* A VC firm's future depends on its ability to generate returns. If it does not have a strong portfolio or meaningful exits, the firm may not be on solid ground. In addition, if a VC firm is struggling, the partners may be focused on issues, such as the survival of their firm, interpersonal conflicts, or short-term exits, that are different from what you want them to be focused on.

A combination of previously mentioned individual attributes, the VCs firm's financial strength, its stability, and its stature can deliver value to your startup. But many CEOs get caught up in the flamboyance of a resume. Greg Gottesman, managing director of Madrona Venture Group, points out that entrepreneurs often are looking for VC board members with incredible resumes, but that's a big mistake. "If I can find a truly prestigious VC board member, that's great. But when you're choosing a board member, it should also be someone who has the time to address critical issues when they arise. Often, founders choose out-of-town board members or board members that are highly prestigious but are unavailable when needed."

If you want a deeper and more thorough explanation of the dynamics within a VC firm, *Venture Deals: Be Smarter Than Your Lawyer and Venture Capitalist* covers it in the chapter titled "How Venture Capital Firms Work."

INDEPENDENT BOARD MEMBERS

Most board members in a startup represent either the investors or the founders. An independent board member represents neither group. Optimally, an independent board member will be unbiased and ultimately concerned about the company rather than the specific interests of a founder or investor. The composition of a startup board is often balanced between the investors and the entrepreneurs with at least one independent board member.

Data show that board control is typically shared more than 60 percent of the time with a third-party independent director holding the tie-breaking vote.[4] If the independent director is well respected and has the trust of both the investor and founder board members, he can often act as a mediator or voice of reason when conflict arises. Thomas Porter, EDF Ventures cofounder, points out, "The independent board member is the third leg of the stool—the investors and founders can often get in situations which call for an objective view. Without the third leg of the stool, you cannot have much-needed stability."

Founders and investors should invest the time and effort to identify the right independent board member and bring them on board as soon as feasible. Unfortunately, this effort is often deferred, especially early in the life of a company. While early financing documents often provide for an independent director as part of the board, this seat is often left empty due to the excitement of the new relationship, the hurry to get the product out, or the lack of understanding of the value of an outside director.

Andreessen Horowitz general partner Scott Weiss was the founder CEO of IronPort Systems, which was acquired by Cisco in 2007 for $830 million.[5] At the time, IronPort's board consisted of two VCs, two founders (including Scott), and three CEOs of other companies serving as outside board members. Following are Scott's reflections on the composition of his board.

I'm a firm believer that neither the founders nor the VCs should have control of the board. My rule of thumb is that with every VC on the board, you should add an external, independent board member. Often, founders get excited about some crazy idea that makes no sense and want to pivot the whole company around that idea. And VCs have various financial pressures. The founder who has never been in business before and a VC who is stereotypical each could be wrong. I counsel entrepreneurs to seek an independent voice on your board. The more independent voices, preferably CEOs, that you have on the board, the more it levels the conversation of the board. VCs are much less likely to pontificate especially when you have a few CEOs who have "been there, done that." The least dysfunctional board meetings I've been in are the ones that have CEOs sitting around the table.

Scott Weiss, Partner, Andreessen Horowitz

Union Square Ventures partner Fred Wilson, who served on the Return Path board with Scott for many years, where Scott was an outside director, adds to this viewpoint.

As a company moves from founder control to investor control, the notion of an independent director crops up. An independent director is a director who does not represent either the founder or the investors. I am a big fan of independent directors. Boards that are full of vested interests are not good boards. The more independent minded the board becomes, the better it usually is. I would argue that an investor-controlled board is the worst possible situation. Investors usually have a narrow set of interests that involve how much money they are going to make (or lose) on their investment. It is the rare investor who takes a broader and more holistic view of the company. So while investor directors are a necessary evil in many companies, they should not dominate or control the board. The founder should control the board, and independent directors should control a board where the founder does not control the company.

Fred Wilson, Partner, Union Square Ventures, www.avc.com/a_vc/2012/03/
the-board-of-directors-selecting-electing-evolving.html

This perspective isn't limited to VCs and entrepreneurs turned VC. Will Herman, a serial entrepreneur turned angel investor, explains in more depth.

I've been a director of over 20 companies so far. I think I was a good director on most of those boards, and I knew that I sucked on at least a couple of them. Several of the companies were publicly traded, but the vast majority were private, small, venture-backed companies. On those boards, I was (and still am at a few) usually the only outside director, that is, a board member who is not affiliated with the company as an employee or a substantial investor.

Like all directors, the outside director helps guide the company by taking a participative role in strategy setting; helps the management team make high-level financial decisions; contributes to the setting of overall direction; determines compensation when appropriate; asks loads of probing questions; and advises the CEO when asked and, as needed, when not asked. That said, none of that is where an outside director, especially of a startup, spends most of his or her time.

Outside directors can fill a unique role on the board. Since they are not big investors (they may have a small stake in the company), they have no other duties other than those to the company, its management team, and its shareholders. Unlike the investors on the board, the outside director has no limited partners to report back to or any other type of investment agenda. Additionally, the outside board member will often be the most operationally experienced board member. Where the investors on the board have seen and done a lot, most often they have neither the in-depth management and/or domain expertise that an outsider chosen for that wisdom brings to the table.

This combination of independence and knowledge not only brings a different type of guidance to the startup's team, but also helps to build a strong relationship between the CEO and the outside board member—less intimidating and lower risk. It's that relationship that is the basis for the outside board member's real role, which includes:

- CEO coach/mentor/therapist.
- Mediator of differences between investors and management (and sometimes, between investors).
- First-line adviser when things aren't going well.
- Nonjudgmental sounding board for early ideas.
- Purveyor of information and decisions from the board to the management team and from the management team to the board.
- Provider of specific advice about the approach to the target market.
- Reviewer of initial compensation proposals for the management team.
- First line of communication with the board outside the boardroom.
- Adviser to the CEO when HR issues and changes come up.
- Overall feedback to the CEO on how a board meeting went and what should be changed for subsequent meetings.
- The first two items on this list—CEO coach and mediator—stand out strongly in my experience. This is where an outside director often adds the most value and spends the most time.

Creating and running a startup can be stressful and time consuming. By its very nature, it will stretch the knowledge, ability, and energy of the CEO and management team. Since the outside director should have loads of operational experience and will often have specific industry knowledge, chances are he has experienced almost everything the CEO will go through. Who better to listen, advise, and counsel?

Perhaps even more important is that outside board members will be less intimidating for the CEO to talk to—and open up to about concerns—since the CEO doesn't have to worry about jeopardizing the funding of the company. More common ground can be found, a broader range of topics can be covered, and a deeper relationship can be built. Ultimately, the outside board member becomes the go-to adviser, working on operational issues and opportunities as well as emotional issues when the CEO or team members feel crushed under the day-to-day stress of running the company.

Another important role of the outside director is that of the mediator or synthesizer of the parochial opinions of the insiders—those who invested in the company. Often, this means bridging the gap between the management team and the investors in the company. Once in a while, it means trying to find common ground between investors. It doesn't happen often, but sometimes there are just some deep, fundamental disagreements between the management team and the company's investors. These would likely work themselves out over time, but that ends up being a waste of energy for all involved. Even if the outside director strongly supports one of the perspectives, since they are close to both sides, they are in a unique position to cut through to the core issues and find agreement much faster. Sometimes that means going to the mat to support the management team, and sometimes it means working with the CEO to help them understand the nuances and importance of the investor's position.

As a CEO, I always appreciated the outside directors who sat on my boards. Even when their energy was directed at talking me off the ledge (i.e., I was wrong and needed to be shown the path), someone stepping in, holding my hand, and offering me a different perspective on a particular issue was a huge help. I truly valued having the person and role on my board. Similarly, I knew the outside director was working with my investors to try to find common ground when she felt that the management team was in the right, which made me feel like I had an additional strong voice helping me out with important board-level issues.

A well-chosen outside board member can be a huge addition to a CEO's extended team. She can be a good board member, for sure, but she will spend the majority of her time doing so much more.

Will Herman, Angel Investor

THE ROLE OF AN EXECUTIVE CHAIRMAN

Earlier, we discussed the role of a chair, or lead director, on the board. However, there is another type of chairman who is an active member of the management team. Often, the *executive chairman* is a founder of the company and can often be the largest noninvestor shareholder of the business. An executive chairman can be a full- or part-time employee of the company, but in either case he has a significant role in some aspect of the company.

Few people are as articulate about, or as successful in, the role of executive chairman as Reid Hoffman. Reid co-founded LinkedIn and serves as its executive chairman, and is also a partner at Greylock, an extremely successful venture capital firm, which is a major investor in LinkedIn. Reid explains how he approaches the role of executive chairman:

A few years after I co-founded LinkedIn in 2003, I decided to shift my role in the company from CEO to executive chairman. Except for a few months in 2009, when I briefly returned to the role of CEO, that's the title I've held since 2007.

While there are a fairly clear-cut set of roles and responsibilities attached to the job of "CEO," an executive chairman at company X may play a much different role than the executive chairman at company Y. It's a nebulous job title. It all depends on the company in question and the person fulfilling the position.

I made the shift because LinkedIn was itself in a state of transition, shifting from a startup to a growth-stage company that was rapidly adding employees. While I love articulating a product vision and other facets of early-stage entrepreneurship, LinkedIn had reached that point where whoever was acting as CEO needed to devote an increasing amount of time to organization building, international expansion, developing scalable business process—those kinds of things.

Assuming the role of executive chairman has allowed me to continue playing a highly involved role at LinkedIn in terms of developing its overall strategy and being involved in key projects, while at the same time handing off the operations to the CEO. (Our first CEO after I moved to executive chairman was Dan Nye, who fulfilled that role from 2007 to 2009. Our current CEO, Jeff Weiner, joined the company in the middle of 2009.)

In the majority of publicly traded companies in the United States, the CEO functions as the chairman of the board as well. But non-CEO chairs have become more popular in recent years, and that means there are two other options for board leadership: an executive chairman or a non-executive chairman.

An executive chairman fulfills all the duties that a non-executive chairman does, but also tends to be more involved than a classic board member. She has a greater role in developing and analyzing specific strategic projects at the company. In my own case, for example, I continue to play a role in developing LinkedIn's product road map, talent management, and corporate and business development. I'm still an employee of the company, I remain on various internal e-mail mailing lists, and I maintain an office at LinkedIn, where I go at least a few days a week. (To reiterate, the role of executive chairman can truly vary; as the co-founder and largest individual shareholder of LinkedIn, I am more involved in discussions around values and culture than traditional executive chairmen.)

As active as I remain at LinkedIn, however, the division between what I do and what our CEO Jeff Weiner does is very clear. Ultimately, the buck stops with Jeff. If Jeff makes a decision, the decision has been made. Period. While I try to offer Jeff honest and candid advice, and even challenge his ideas on occasion, he has operational control over the company. The CEO works for the company, not for the executive chairman or the board. (The board hires and fires the CEO, but it's a mistake to assume the CEO reports to the board in the same the way an employee reports to his manager.)

Unlike Jeff, people don't report to me. I act in an advisory role, not an operational one, and that's by careful design. If your CEO is spending time worried that you're trying to undermine his authority, or if employees go to the executive chairman when they get an answer they don't like from the CEO, you are probably not doing a very good job as executive chairman. An executive chairman should never override the organizational chain of command.

Not surprisingly, trust is the key factor in the relationship between an executive chairman and the CEO. After all, neither "works" explicitly for the other, so trust and shared commitment to the company's vision are what make the relationship productive. As executive chairman, my most important job is helping Jeff do the best job he can do. Sometimes this means helping recruit and retain great people. Sometimes this means helping launch international expansion or a new product. Always it means being a great partner to Jeff and the entire executive team, so that together, with our thousands of LinkedIn colleagues around the world, we advance our vision of bringing economic opportunity to every professional in the global workforce.

Reid Hoffman, Executive Chairman, LinkedIn

BOARD OBSERVERS

Many boards have *board observers* who have the right to sit in, observe, and participate in portions of the board meeting, but do not have formal board roles or responsibilities. Observers also do not get to vote on board matters. Often, an observer is a VC or a co-founder of the company.

In an effort to limit the size of a board, many companies grant observer seats to later-stage investors. In other cases, in an effort to limit control, strategic investors get observer rights instead of actual board seats. Some strategic investors prefer this, as it minimizes any liabilities their corporation may face due to actions of the board and individual board members.

VC partners who want a junior member of their firm, either an associate or a younger partner, to participate in the board meetings often also ask for an observer right in addition to a board seat. In the best case, these junior members of the firm don't show up without the VC board member partner and never end up being a "proxy board member" for the actual board member. Instead, they are observers, listening to what is going on and helping support their VC partner when appropriate.

Early in the life of a company, more than one founder may be on the board. However, as the board grows, the number of founders on the board is often reduced. While there is often a founder seat and a CEO seat, the CEO may no longer be a founder, or there may be additional founders that have observer rights.

Observers don't have a right to be in the *closed session of the board*, also referred to as the *executive session*. Observers will respect this, but it can be taken to a ridiculous level, where there are two separate board meetings— the first one with the observers, which ends up being a high-level reporting session, and then the one with just the board members, which is the actual board meeting.

While startups don't have to have observer board members, they can bring great value to your startup. Tim Petersen, managing director of Arboretum Ventures, was a board observer early on in his career. "I was able to help the CEO of a portfolio company in testing a market hypothesis—it was heavy lifting at a very critical time in the company's trajectory. We did not get hung up on titles but focused on what the company needed."

While an entrepreneur may believe he is managing the size of his board through the use of observer rights, we've sat in boardrooms with 20 people or more, where only 5 of them are board members. We've experienced VC firms who use their observer rights to "bring power to the board meeting," where instead of one board seat, the observer seat is used to effectively have two board members. And we've been in situations where it's confusing who is a board member and who isn't.

Ultimately, it's the lead director's and the CEO's responsibility to manage the observer dynamic. Creating a clear set of rules and expectations and then living by them is the best way to maximize the value of the observers' involvement.

YOUR LAWYER

A great lawyer, especially an outside counsel who is experienced with working with startups, can be a great addition to the boardroom. While outside counsel rarely takes a seat on the board, including them actively in all board activity is powerful, and in some cases necessary. If your company is large enough to have a general counsel on your team, including them in all board meetings and board activity is also important.

But your lawyer isn't just there to focus and pay attention to "legal stuff." Following are some thoughts from Cooley LLP partner Mike Platt on the role that a lawyer can play in the growth of a company.

Startup lawyers can and do play a material role in helping grow a seed-stage company through an IPO or exit transaction. And providing good legal advice is just "table stakes" to being effective in that role. Effective startup attorneys need to be business-minded, recognize that early-stage companies must remain nimble, and take greater business risk to achieve greater returns. But that concept should not be confused with simply ignoring the legal and business issues facing the company, but rather should be thoughtfully and transparently discussed. Judged against this backdrop, a good startup layer earns her keep by assisting boards and companies with creative (and hopefully simple) solutions to complex business interests. To accomplish this goal, attorneys need the support of good board members and access to decision makers and the decision-making process early enough to have an impact. If you don't trust your lawyer to be engaged early or believe that "bringing the lawyers in early" will be expensive, you have the wrong lawyer.

I have assembled a short list of objectives a board member should expect of counsel, as well as be proactive in helping counsel achieve through effective communication, support, and board access:

Represent the company and stockholders "as a whole." Counsel must provide a neutral and dispassionate perspective regarding legal matters and transactions. In many venture-backed companies, counsel is often the only person in the boardroom without a direct and material financial interest in the company. Balancing the relationship of differing financial interests is tough but is one of the most value-added roles for outside counsel. Transactions often have conflicting interests between classes of stock, investors with different liquidity time horizons, and management versus investment interests. A board counselor seeks to gain the trust of multiple factions by facilitating open discussion of those potential conflicts and helps structure transactions that have greater likelihood of aligning those interests to the maximum extent possible.

Participate in board meetings, but don't "hijack" the dialogue for legal issues. Board meetings are a time for the development of strategy, and except in the most material transactions, not for the analysis of detailed and nuanced legal risks. And the responsibility for keeping the dialogue at the strategy level lies with both counsel and the board. While in many instances attorneys can be the guilty party for hijacking the agenda, often board members suggest concerns with "legal issues" as a way to avoid conflict with management on more fundamental business concerns with a particular transaction.

Engage with both management and the board collectively and independently. A lawyer should build relationships with both the board and management. She will only be effective if trusted by all constituencies. To this end, management team members need to encourage and facilitate outside counsel's ability to develop that relationship, and non-management board members need to both demand direct access to counsel and be responsive to counsel's request for engagement with them on matters, especially where they involve management conflicts of interest (e.g., compensation matters and related-party transactions).

Coach management on what should go to the board and how to help them make good decisions. This may be the first time an entrepreneur has worked with a board. Offer assistance and coaching to the entrepreneur as to when and how to engage with a board. There are times when matters should be dealt with in a properly convened board meeting, times when a matter should not be on the board meeting agenda until management has had independent discussions with each board member, and times when something is not ready for a board discussion at all. Boards should expect their startup lawyer to be helpful to the CEO in making some of these judgments and coach the entrepreneur to improve their ability to manage these board processes.

Keep the cap table clean. Emerging growth companies have complex cap tables with multiple classes of stock, options for employee, and adviser equity and warrants for debt financing and partner incentives. In fact, the average emerging growth company has a more complex capital structure than most small public companies or private equity-backed enterprises with substantially great internal staff to assist with cap table management. As a result, outside counsel should play an important role in initially maintaining good capitalization and other corporate records, including effective records of board and stockholder approvals. Bad record keeping, or poorly managed capitalization material, account for more "legal budget overruns" than all other problems combined.

Be open to criticism, don't be defensive, and request constructive feedback. Lawyers pride themselves on, and generally achieve, a high degree of perfection. At the same time, business transactions aren't perfect, exigencies often drive suboptimal results, and outright mistakes sometimes occur. Your lawyer should be open to hearing those concerns and your board should have a mechanism to openly provide that dialogue as a means to improve the quality and consistency of the legal process. Generally, all constituencies learn something from a well-developed feedback loop. And, as with all feedback, provide it early. Try to avoid coupling it with the negotiation of a bill. I'm not saying that billing adjustments aren't a reasonable request for unproductive services, but you can imagine that when feedback is always coupled with a request for a discount, it loses its credibility as a legitimate request to improve the quality of the legal services.

Never, ever, bend the truth with the board, or be anything less than appropriately transparent. I rarely have observed an attorney lie, but I have observed many willing to be less than transparent. You should demand absolute transparency with outside counsel and seek to protect them from board or management criticism when they are living up to this obligation. Above all, the lawyer must be a trusted adviser to accomplish many of the objectives discussed above.

Mike Platt, Partner, Cooley LLP

SHOULD GENDER DIVERSITY MATTER?

While startup boards seldom have the luxury of focusing on diversity, your goal should be to stimulate rapid growth through creative ferment. If all the board members are nodding in unison to everything you say, something is missing. You don't need groupthink; you need creative and challenging minds. Focus on getting the best people to offer you varying viewpoints; these perspectives can come through diversity by gender, age, experience, and cultural background. This diversity can be a powerful asset in any startup board; however, such diversified boards are often an exception at very early stages of the startup's journey.

Gender diversity is a particularly powerful dynamic. Over the past decade, a huge effort has been under way to recruit female board members to public company boards. The image of a boardroom filled with white men has changed for public companies, and the annual *Fortune* magazine issue on boards illustrates this beautifully with creative photographs of the best public company boards. However, gender diversity has been slow to come to private companies, especially early-stage ones.

Cowboy Ventures partner Aileen Lee says that it makes good business sense to have women on your board since they make buying decisions and bring a different mindset to the equation then men. Aileen writes:

Less than 10% of Silicon Valley boards have women representation. Companies with gender diversity at the top drive better financial performance on multiple measures—for example, 36% better stock price growth and 46% better return on equity. And, studies show the more women, the better the results. This is likely because teams with more females demonstrate higher collective intelligence and better problem solving ability. So it's probably not a coincidence the world's most admired companies have more women on their boards than the average company.[6]

Successful startups have twice as many women in senior positions, according to Dow Jones Venture Source 2011. Tech startups use 40 percent less capital in their early years when led by women, and have a higher probability of survival, according to data collected by Cindy Padnos, managing partner of Illuminate Ventures. Cindy says, "With startup boards typically being made up of founders and investors and the fact that less than 10% of either founders or VC partners are women, it's definitely challenging to build a diverse startup board. Most people have not even begun to think about how to establish diversity on these boards." A Credit Suisse report from August 2012, "Gender Diversity and Performance," shows that in an analysis of 2,360 publicly traded companies using over 14,000 data points, companies with more than three women on the board had a market cap three times higher than those with no women.

Why don't we see gender diversity on startup boards? Let's start with the concept of *unconscious bias*. Consider Abbie Conant, who applied for the position of a trombonist at the Munich Philharmonic. Candidates were asked to conduct a blind audition, and Abbie was judged the best among 33 candidates, of which 32 were men. Yet when she stepped out from behind the screen, the judges were shocked—a woman? The judges decided, once they saw she was a woman, that she did not have enough physical strength. Or nerves. Or empathy. She could not play because she did not have enough lung capacity. But Abbie was a fighter, and after 13 years of legal battles, the German courts ruled that Abbie be placed in the same pay and seniority group as all of her male solo-wind colleagues.

Accepting the status quo is often a default behavior in business. Get Satisfaction CEO Wendy Lea points out that "most founders are men and most investors are men," which results in a self-referential good-old-boys network problem unless you make a proactive effort to do something different. While the bias may be unconscious, there is a cost associated with it in lower performance and creativity. Consider this 20 percent bias: in surveys, as many as 80 percent of startup women think diversity offers better problem solving and improves innovation. Yet only 60 percent of the startup men felt the same. On the flip side, 80 percent of men felt that they are addressing diversity in the workplace but only 60 percent of women agreed. That 20 percent gap on both those counts signifies meaningful unconscious bias.[7]

Cindy Padnos gives us a straightforward example. While serving on a startup board, the question of adding a new board member came up. This was a male-dominated board, with Cindy being the lone female board member at the time. Several candidates were proposed. Cindy recommended the name of a very well qualified woman, who the rest of the board members readily agreed was the best target candidate and subsequently was recruited to join the board. Cindy pointed out that "there was no intentional bias—it was more of a top-of-the-mind issue—everyone readily agreed to bring her on, but no one, including the other board members who knew her better, thought of adding her or adding any other woman candidate."

Unconscious bias sneaks into many different decisions, with gender diversity on boards simply being one of them. As an entrepreneur and board member, working hard to eliminate unconscious bias will make your business stronger.

Remember that we aren't talking about gender diversity for the sake of gender parity, but rather improving the quality and increasing the performance of your board. Wendy Lea says, "It's a sign of an evolved CEO who balances out the yin and the yang. At the end of the day, we are talking about the feminine energy and masculine energy—how these two can help the startup grow and become successful." Google Ventures partner Shanna Tellerman, an entrepreneur who sold her VC-backed startup to Autodesk, experienced this first hand. "I had a great board—the men would often make sure that we never missed the big-picture thinking, yet some of the granular level of attention to detail was brought by women on my board. In the end, it was my responsibility to make sure I kept all of them aligned." For Jim Dai, CEO of CalmSee, having a female board member was a requirement. "All my life, I have had very positive experiences while working for or reporting to women. There is no question of their competence or ability to help, yet we see this imbalance." Hoopla CEO Mike Smalls states, "It says a lot about the company when you see balance. It's not good to have a skewed ratio. My board members, who include a woman, have been good, down to earth, and helpful. They care about our success and provide real value. If there is such a myth about women on startup boards, we need to bust it quickly."

Those who have had experience with female board members spoke overwhelmingly of the value received, especially in the context of being accountable around performance. Lucy Sanders, CEO of the National Center for Women & Information Technology, has been on a number of boards and reminds us that "while it's about performance at all times, women can raise some issues quickly." Lucy pointed out a board situation where on an all-male board other than Lucy, the VP of sales continued to miss his targets. Yet he doled out great punch lines and smooth talk. The board went along with this until Lucy, the solo woman on the board, raised her hand and challenged the performance of the VP of sales. That VP of sales was ultimately fired.

BEING RICH AND KING

Occasionally, founders have retained both board-level control and economics that last through an IPO of the company. A few, like Mark Zuckerberg, have become, in Noam Wasserman's words, both rich and king. To do this, you need to have a large stock position and voting control, which can be achieved even if you don't own more than 50 percent of the company.

In the case of Facebook, the company created two classes of shares before it went public. At the time of the IPO, Zuckerberg owned 18 percent of the company. However, he owned Class B shares, which had 10 votes to every one vote of the Class A shares that were being sold to the public in the IPO. In addition, even though he only owned 28 percent of the Class B shares, several other founders (who were also Class B shareholders) entered into a voting agreement with Zuckerberg that gave him voting control over 57 percent of the Class B shares and greater than 50 percent voting control over the overall company.

This is not a new approach. Google went public in 2004 with a similar structure, and numerous media companies, such as Viacom and News Corp, have dual-class share structures as public companies. More recently, tech IPOs from the 2011–2012 class, including LinkedIn, Groupon, Yelp, and Zynga, also used dual-class share structures.

James Surowiecki, financial columnist for *The New Yorker*, writes:

> One of the problems besetting modern business is the short-termism of big institutional investors. In the postwar era, most shareholders were individual investors who held on to stocks for ages and exerted little pressure on companies. Executives didn't have to worry

about quarterly earnings and had the freedom to invest in long-term research and development. In today's market, by contrast, investors are far more aggressive in pressuring companies to hit their numbers. . . . Investors now have very short-term horizons. The average annual turnover of a mutual fund portfolio is a hundred percent, and for a hedge fund portfolio around three hundred percent.[8]

It's important to note that this dual-class share structure is not necessarily put in place simply to be king or massage a young CEO's ego. Instead, it's being used to manage the short-term view of many public-market investors, who often are myopic and seek magical results every quarter. This structure can be a defense mechanism in this day of activist shareholders, deterring these investors from exerting inappropriate operating pressure on the company.

CHAPTER FOUR

RECRUITING BOARD MEMBERS

The process of identifying, recruiting, and vetting board members is similar to that of adding someone to your senior leadership team. Great people don't randomly show up and join the team. They often aren't the first obvious choice. And you need to work hard to get them.

THE VALUE OF GOOD BOARD MEMBERS

Before you start searching for a new board member, it's useful to define the characteristics that you are looking for in this person. While this will vary based on the stage of your company, following are some examples of skills you may be looking for:

Customer development. In the early stage of a business, some of the major goals include understanding customer needs, developing a product that addresses these needs, determining a go-to-market approach, and figuring out pricing. This process is nonlinear and fraught with challenges, pivots, and failures. A board member who understands methodologies like customer development and lean startup and has experience developing and launching products is invaluable.

Product development. While your board members won't be writing code or actually working on product development, a board member with a technical background and real product development experience can offer insights, provide coaching to the product team, and help you understand what is needed to build and ship your product faster.

Business model development. Many startups struggle early on in their evolution with choices around the business model such as freemium versus paid pricing, direct versus indirect channels, or license versus subscription revenue models. In addition to helping define the best approach, board members can help with partner development. VictorOps CEO Todd Vernon says, "Early on, one of our board members knew a major channel partner that resulted in really propelling the revenue dramatically after we added him to the board. We got that relationship really early on. We would have never gotten that deal because we were too small at the time to partner with this large company."

Team building. As a CEO, you should be continuously building your team. In addition to identifying and recruiting people, board members can help you develop hiring techniques, figure out how to integrate new team members into the business, and help create a culture that reflects the goals and values of your business.

Fundraising. Board members can be integral to fundraising by defining the funding strategy, identifying potential investors, making introductions, and adding credibility to the fundraising process simply through their involvement. Understanding how your directors think about additional rounds of funding is important, as there are many inherent conflicts one must balance when he is both a board member and investor; these are discussed later in the book.

HELPING YOU THINK BIG OR KILLING YOUR COMPANY

A board member can be an incredible asset to your company, or he can potentially destroy it. Let's look at two examples—first, a good one from Ryan McIntyre, managing director of the Foundry Group, about the positive impact of Khosla Ventures managing director Vinod Khosla on Excite, a company that Ryan cofounded.

Early in the days of Excite we received an acquisition offer from a pre-IPO company that we turned down. At the time we received the offer, Excite was only the six founders, and we hadn't yet raised any outside money beyond about $15,000 from our parents. We had to decide between selling the company and taking a venture capital investment from Vinod Khosla of Kleiner Perkins and Geoff Yang of IVP. As we were deliberating on our decision, Vinod invited us to his amazing home in Portola Valley and told us "if you guys turn down the acquisition offer, I'm going to do everything I can to make sure your company becomes hugely successful, and that you guys make vastly more money. And to do that, you have to think big." That meant a lot to us.

At the time of this discussion in late 1994, the acquisition offer was for around $3 million. After refusing to sell out, Excite grew, went public, and merged with another public company in a transaction worth $6.7 billion.

Shortly after the launch of Excite.com in October 1995, Vinod observed that Excite was taking part in the birth and rapid expansion of a new form of media, and that based on the growth rate of the site, our user base would soon reach millions and then tens of millions of users. He pointed out that companies like NBC, CBS, and ABC had audiences of similar scale and that Excite had the potential to have the impact and value of major media companies like the TV networks. Having the perspective to see this and encouraging us to have the audacity to think at that scale was tremendously valuable to a company that at the time had maybe two dozen employees, the majority of whom were on their first or second job and in their mid-20s.

Ryan McIntyre, Managing Director, Foundry Group

In contrast, following is a story from Rally Software CEO Tim Miller about a board member who helped sink a company.

In an earlier software services company that I was part of, I was a principal. We were three years into the business and had about 40 employees. The founders had a blend of technology and marketing expertise. They got restless about their growth to the next level but had a setback with one of their major accounts, as they hit some scaling issues, and they were looking for answers. At that size, a company can easily hit the valley of death.

This guy comes in from an investment banking background, and boy, could he sell! In desperation, the founders brought him in as a board member. The founders were getting exhausted and were looking for someone who could not only save this ship but also grow it and play a strategic role in helping them move forward. The founders let him in and gave him equity. Over a period of nine months, this board member took control of the company and got a pretty lavish expense account.

The founders failed to heed the first warning sign. When they did background checks, he dropped a lot of names but when they called them he went ballistic and said, "You go through me," and basically shut that down. He was prone to power play and was also kind of a Mr. Know-it-all—very slick.

Soon thereafter he got in an operational role and had an inappropriate relationship with at least four employees. The company went into a downward spiral and was sold a year or so later. I am still amazed at how he did it—he was a silver-tongued devil. We all wanted to believe in him.

The hard lesson was that in desperation, we picked a guy who had no domain expertise, no integrity, and no operational expertise. That decision cost us the company.

There are a fair number of wannabe board members out there stalking early-stage companies. They extract money as opposed to adding value. Be careful of those who just fly into your life without any connection to your ecosystem.

Tim Miller, CEO, Rally Software

CHARACTERISTICS AND SKILLS OF A BOARD MEMBER

A board is composed of three different types of board members: investors, members of the management team, and independent board members. Return Path CEO Matt Blumberg writes, "Take the process of building the board as seriously as you take building your executive team—both in terms of your time and the overall composition of the board, not just a given board member."

Consider the characteristics of a board member along the dimensions of integrity, intellectual acuity, and emotional quotient, which are summarized in Table 4.1.

Make sure that the integrity is uncompromising. Warren Buffett once remarked, "Somebody once said that in looking for people to hire, you look for three qualities: integrity, intelligence, and energy. And if they don't have the first, the other two will kill you. Think about it; it's true. If you hire somebody without the first, you really want him to be dumb and lazy."

TABLE 4.1 Positive and Negative Characteristics of a Board Member

Characteristics	What You Want	What You Should Avoid
Integrity	Honest, transparent, loyal, and steadfast. Takes responsibility for actions. Known for fairness.	Shifty, unpredictable, and unclear who he is really working for. Can turn against you at any time.
Intellectual Acuity	Bold yet measured. Calls out your flawed thinking. Challenges you appropriately. Knows market challenges and opportunities, learns by doing, gathers inputs from various sources, and draws meaningful conclusions.	Bravado exceeds intellectual abilities. Offers clichés and quick fixes. Shoots from the hip and disregards the consequences of his actions. Agrees to everything you say.
Emotional Quotient	Nurturing, mellow, yet does not compromise on discipline. A guide, a mensch, and a mentor. Does not play the game but acts as a coach. Respects people. Engaged for the long haul.	Sucks up your energy. Creates artificial emergencies. Finds out your flaws when you are most vulnerable and hurts you when you least expect. Screamer. High maintenance.

According to Jeffrey Bussgang, general partner at Flybridge Capital Partners, the personalities of a board member fall into one of three categories—the domain expert, the cheerleader, or the truth teller:[1]

The domain expert. She knows the domain of the business inside out, provides relevant constructive feedback, is well connected, and empathetic. While great in the details of the business, the downside of the domain expert is that she has a tendency to miss the big picture, especially when broad market shifts occur.

The cheerleader. Always encouraging and supportive, he's the king of the pep talk, especially when things are rough. While the "Nice Job" and "Love Ya" statements help, they wear thin, especially when the chips are down and you need objective, hard, critical thinking.

The truth teller. The truth teller is brutally honest. Some deliver the message sharply, others are gentle, but a great truth teller is an invaluable person to have on the board.

Each board member will have different strengths and experiences across a wide range of skills. See Table 4.2 for some examples.

TABLE 4.2 Different Skills of a Board Member

Skills	Great	Fair	Terrible
Entrepreneurial	Has started several companies and hired A players. Knows all about customer discovery and validation. Can surround herself with giants.	Worked with larger companies. Has a consulting or other background that is not an obvious fit.	Has fantasized about startups but has never been remotely involved with one. Unable to prioritize or deal with ambiguity.
Domain Expertise	Has hands-on experience in building products in similar markets.	Market awareness via secondary sources. Lacks depth, but may have potential.	Knows the obvious. Asks random and annoying questions like "What's your mobile strategy?"
Business Development	Has developed a value proposition, a sales pitch for a new product in an emerging market, identified early adopters, closed orders, and generated revenue.	Has sold products in established and mature markets. Met quotas. Does not necessarily have the creativity or persistence to sell new products.	Looks forward to having coffee, accumulating frequent flyer miles, and having fancy lunches.
Financial	Has raised multiple rounds of capital leading to a successful exit. Generated returns for all stakeholders.	Understands financials but has not raised capital, dealt with venture capitalists (VCs), sold a company, or taken one public.	Thinks a balance sheet is used while doing the downward-facing dog yoga pose.
Legal	Understands contracts and legal and regulatory guidelines around finance, taxation, and employment.	Demonstrates baseline business judgment acumen. Has never been sued.	Does not realize what can land you in jail. Naïve.

The characteristics that make a great board member vary, but experienced CEOs who have been through multiple boards often have strong opinions about what is minimally needed. Not surprisingly, trust, transparency, experience, and responsiveness consistently top the list. Following is an excellent view from Andreessen Horowitz partner Scott Weiss:

"There was never any trust there. He was constantly conspiring behind my back with the other board members. At the board meetings, it was clear that he was leading a bunch of side conversations. . ."

I heard this quote from a CEO I had called for a backdoor reference on a potential board member for IronPort. It instantly made me realize the importance of transparency between a CEO and his board. If I were to totally suck at being a CEO, I wanted someone who would have the hard conversation with me. How else does someone learn and improve?

As a first-time CEO, I wasn't sure if I would scale to run IronPort long term. But I wanted a legitimate shot at it. And I wanted a board member that considered the company's interest first, but was also committed to helping me become a better CEO.

I will never forget that backdoor reference because it made me think twice about the fundamental skills and characteristics I wanted in a board member. Early on, it became clear that transparency and the ability to provide honest feedback were paramount. I learned this through receiving instant and honest feedback following every board meeting (a healthy board practice). When this was coupled with annual 360 performance evaluations I always knew where I stood. The feedback was crucial for my growth.

In addition to transparency and feedback, through my own personal CEO journey, I came to realize that the following represents table stakes for the best board members:

> *Experience.* I wanted someone who had been there, done that. In addition to the investors, I went out of my way to recruit three CEOs to the IronPort board because I wanted to surround myself with people who could help steer me around common potholes and would be unflappable as things were going haywire. Diversity of experience was also very helpful. Some of my board members had been on 50 boards, while others had run large direct sales organizations; both contributed in completely different ways. If given a choice, I don't see why any entrepreneur would take a term sheet from a VC with little or no board or operating experience.
>
> *Sharp opinion.* Quiet is not helpful. A Melvin Milquetoast who sits there nodding his head at meetings is not helpful. I wanted someone who consistently contributed meaningfully and constructively to the conversation, however wide ranging it became. Every board member slot is an opportunity to find someone truly amazing who will speak up and help you build your business. The traditional "financial expert" as a board member essentially compromises a valuable seat with a former CFO or accountant who rarely contributes outside of their domain. It's worth

working hard to find a CFO that later became a CEO or interviewing hard for a financial expert who really contributes. The thorniest business problems will surface at the board meetings, and the different, sharp opinions help to better explore the poles of the arguments to make better decisions.

Responsive. Board members need to respond to texts within hours and e-mails or phone calls within 24 hours—no excuses. Things move fast at startups, and when I needed help with a lawsuit, contract, employee situation, or financing, I wanted to have a damn batphone with my board members. Yes, I realize that I was not in the business of saving lives, but the difference between landing a rock star candidate or closing a round often depended on the timeliness of a board member's response.

Does real shit. Being on a board is not just about showing up for the meetings. A board member needs to materially contribute to the success of the business. This includes making numerous introductions to potential customers, partners, and employee candidates. This is in addition to being available to interview/sell employee candidates, coach management team members, speak at sales kickoffs, or just about anything reasonable that a CEO asks you to do to help the business.

I once had a venture capitalist explain to me that a board doesn't have many options when it comes to affecting the direction of the company—that if you don't agree with where the CEO is leading the company, you basically have two levers: (1) threaten to fire the CEO, or (2) fire the CEO. He also added that the former gets pulled much more often than the latter. This describes well the authoritarian and adversarial nature of many CEO-to-board relationships. Given the makeup of most boards, where most of the members lack the practical experience to help coach the CEO, the lever approach is not all that surprising. But like any bad relationship, it's something to avoid.

The best board members aren't elected by default. CEOs that set themselves up with their choice of board member—which means getting more than one term sheet and doing extensive reference checking—are better off. You want to find a coach, not a lever puller.

Scott Weiss, Partner, Andreessen Horowitz

While this may seem like a daunting set of criteria, do not compromise. As Matt Blumberg states, "Cast your net wide."

RECRUITING BOARD MEMBERS

The search for a new board member, like the search for any addition to your team, is a process. While you typically will start with people you know—other entrepreneurs, your investors, attorneys, or recruiters—to get introductions, you shouldn't stop there.

Use the characteristics you've come up with to create a list of ideal candidates, including aspirational ones. Then ask yourself these questions about each candidate:

1. What skills does this potential board member have? What would be the single most important contribution this board member could make for my startup over the next year?
2. Will I have the ability to learn and grow under the guidance of this board member?
3. Do I see any conflicts, now or in the near future, that need to be addressed?
4. Will my other board members engage effectively with this person? Are there any known historical conflicts?

Lesa Mitchell, Vice President of Advancing Innovation at the Kauffman Foundation, amplifies this point.

> We tell entrepreneurs to identify the three people who could change the trajectory of their company due to their experience, skills, and networks. If you can find people who bring global knowledge and experience in a related area that will add substantial value to your company, seek them out and sell them on the idea of being an adviser or potentially a board member. If those people are all in your neighborhood, you are clearly not thinking big enough. There is a tendency to fill these valuable board seats with individuals who have never scaled a company. A lesson I acquired over the years is that some mentors and advisers can actually give you harmful advice. You have to be picky! Talk to other entrepreneurs who have scaled companies, talk to C-level executives who have access to the networks and experience you need. This is your company, and the decisions regarding advisers or board members is all on you—make it count.
>
> *Lesa Mitchell, Vice President of Advancing Innovation, Kauffman Foundation*

Once you have your list of prospective candidates, your recruiting process should look similar to the process of recruiting a senior executive to your team. If you know the person, simply reach out directly. If you don't, get a referral from someone you both know. If your only choice is a cold call, try it. Matt Blumberg suggests a direct approach by calling and saying, "I'm the CEO and would like to talk to you about a potential board seat with my company" as an entree to meet with some of the most interesting people in your industry. Blumberg continues, "Interview many people, always face to face and usually multiple times for finalists. Have a few other board members conduct interviews also."

Prepare your pitch, script it, and rehearse it. In your first conversation with a prospective board member, you should be able to address the following questions:

1. What does your startup do?
2. How will it change the world?
3. What role can this person play?
4. Why do you want them to join now?
5. What's in it for them?

Following is a detailed explanation of this process from Matt Blumberg's book *Startup CEO: A Field Guide to Scaling Up Your Business.*

My recruiting process for directors is just as rigorous as what we go through when hiring a new senior executive.

Take the process. Devote as much focus to building your board as to building your executive team—both in terms of your time and in terms of how you think about the overall composition of the board, not just a given board member.

Source broadly. Get a lot of referrals from disparate sources. Reach really high. Remember that asking someone to join your board is a pretty big honor for them, so that ask becomes a good calling card for you. I've had meetings with some amazing CEOs over the years when I've initiated a cold call around the person being a potential board member. Not all have worked out, but almost all of them took the meeting.

Interview many people. Conduct interviews face to face, and conduct multiple interviews with finalists. Also, for finalists, have a few other board members conduct interviews as well.

Check references. As with hiring, check references thoroughly and from multiple sources in different contexts.

Have finalists attend a board meeting. Give the prospective board member extra time to read materials and offer your time to answer questions before the meeting, or even do a one-on-one meeting in person to prep the candidate. You'll get a good first-hand sense of a lot of the top five items this way. You want to see a prospective board member dive into the flow of a conversation in a meeting, even if he or she doesn't know a ton about the material. Someone who is deferential or afraid of saying something dumb or making waves, even during an audition like this, is likely to behave that way once on the board as well.

Have no fear of rejecting potential board members. Even if you like them, even if they are a stretch and someone you consider to be a business hero or mentor, and even after you've already put them on the board—and, yes, even if they're a VC. This is your inner circle. Getting this group right is one of the most important things you can do for your company.

CEOs should go through the same process vetting a future venture investor who will have a board seat. In some ways, it's even more critical to do so for a VC, since it's much harder to remove a poor-performing venture director from your board than it is an independent director. The best venture capitalists always ask you to check their references and usually give you a list of all the CEOs they have ever worked with, with an open invitation to call them. If a prospective venture investor doesn't, ask for it. If they refuse, that's a huge red flag.

Matt Blumberg, CEO, Return Path

While trying to recruit a powerful and successful person to your board may be intimidating, there are many reasons why someone on the receiving end of an invitation to join a board may do it. Many of these reasons are more about the board member than about you or your company. Some successful businesspeople are willing to give before they get and view mentorship as a key part of their role in the world—someone once helped them and they want to pay it forward. Others are interested in staying up to date on an industry by spending some of their time in new startups that are pushing the envelope of new products and services. Yet others simply love to share their experience and give advice. Of course, some are simply motivated by being part of the next big thing and having an opportunity to make some money in the process.

CHECKING REFERENCES

Like any executive recruiting processes, the dance can be complicated. Assume that your prospective board member will want to meet members of the management team, other board members, and do her own diligence on your company. You should use this time to do your diligence on your prospective board member. In addition to talking to CEOs from other boards she has, or is, serving on, try to ascertain whether your prospective board member has enough time for you and your company. Does she have the characteristics and skills you thought she had? Will she fit culturally with the rest of your board?

Examples of questions beyond typical reference checks include:

1. Describe a few tangible examples of how the board member can add value to a startup?
2. How did this board member respond to a challenging situation, such as running out of cash, or a down round?
3. In the context of the board, what are some shortcomings of this person?

Try to keep these questions open-ended. Give the reference a chance to talk and, when you hear something interesting, nudge them along the path for more information. Remember, this isn't a check-the-box exercise; rather, you are looking for detailed information about the person you are considering asking to join a critical part of your team.

As part of the reference-checking process, a candidate should meet with all of your existing board members. You have two goals here: evaluate the potential board member, and give the candidate a chance to ask your board members whatever she wants. View this as a bidirectional reference check, and encourage your board members to be open and candid with the prospective board member.

Once you've decided you want to have the candidate join your board, consider having them attend a board meeting before you extend the formal invitation for them to join. Set the expectation that this is a try-before-you-buy moment—each of you is having one last chance to see if the fit feels right. Have a real board meeting, not a performance for the prospective board member. If there are confidential issues that you don't want to raise in front of her, that's fine, but be clear in advance that there will be a closed session of the board to discuss certain things at the end of the meeting.

Finally, don't be afraid to decide that a prospective board member is not a fit, even at the end of the process. If something comes up that raises a concern from anyone on your board, listen carefully to this and don't be afraid to make the hard decision not to invite the person on the board. Just make sure you communicate clearly with your prospective board member that you've decided there's not a fit at the board level.

PREPARING FOR AN EXPANSION-STAGE BOARD

Scott Maxwell, senior managing director of OpenView Partners, points out that there are seven specific board member personas that are most valuable to an expansion-stage board:[2]

The head of the audit and compensation committee. This person should have previous financial experience (e.g., a former CFO or public auditor), and he or she must work with the CEO, CFO, and other board members to ensure the financial and legal well-being of the business. Additionally, this role is responsible for ensuring that the company's compensation plan is under control and competitive.

The yin to the CEO's yang. A board member who is complementary in some way to the CEO typically fills this role. For instance, if the company's CEO has a sales background, this person might possess a stronger product development or customer experience background. The idea, quite simply, is to identify someone who can help the CEO think creatively and broaden his or her own skill set.

The personification of the company's target market. Typically filled by an independent board member, this is someone who possesses a keen understanding of the company's target market. They tend to possess a strong network of target buyers, and can monitor the pulse of, and trends in, your market. For instance, if your company's primary buyer is the chief marketing officer (CMO) of enterprise software companies, you might recruit a former CMO of a similar company to fill one of your board seats.

The CEO adviser and mentor. While the previous three roles were more externally focused, this role has much more to do with to the company and its CEO's skill set gaps. The CEO adviser and mentor should be a retired CEO that has guided a company through the expansion stage. He can provide the CEO with relevant insight, expertise, and feedback, particularly as the business begins to scale.

The exit strategist. While company executives focus on scaling the business, someone needs to begin to think about the company's strategic direction, economic model, and exit plan. Should the business shoot for a merger or acquisition, or is the better exit strategy an IPO? If a company has accepted outside financing, this role is typically the responsibility of investor board members.

The CEO in the flesh. It might sound obvious to suggest that a company's CEO must also be a board member, but some boards fail to elevate the CEO to the level they should. That's a critical mistake. If the CEO is supposed to command respect and serve as the company's primary leader, how can he or she do that without commanding respect from the board? As a board member, a CEO may not have the same power that he does over his executive team and managers. It's still his job, however, to lead and manage the board.

The chairman of the board. This role might seem obvious, too. Deciding who should fill it, however, can be a tricky issue. The two approaches that companies can typically choose from are either that the CEO is the chair or an independent board member is chairman. In the case where the CEO is also the chair, it's helpful to have another director play the role of the "lead director" to coordinate and communicate with the CEO to make sure all board members are being heard.

CHAPTER FIVE

THE FORMAL STRUCTURE OF THE BOARD

U pon creation of the company, a board is formed. Often, when your company does a financing, the structure of your board will change. This is part of the negotiation around the financing and is usually included in the term sheet discussion. The motivations of the three primary parties—the founders, the investors, and the CEO—are important to understand as they may agree on the financing terms, but may have different views on how the company should evolve.

For example, some investors seek short-term financial returns and may not care much about operational details. However, management is focused on building great products, an awesome user experience, and a huge following of loyal customers. In this case, the investors have a sense of urgency around the financial performance of the company while the entrepreneurs do not understand the rush around the financial dynamics.

This can create a positive tension between the two parties that, if managed well, can ensure appropriate focus, maintain momentum, and establish a system of checks and balances. Conversely, it can create a downward spiral if the alignment among the three parties is poor. Ensuring good alignment goes back to the process of proactively attracting suitable investors and board members (see Figure 5.1).

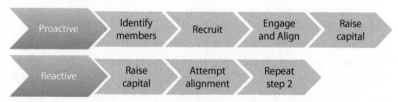

FIGURE 5.1 Two Ways of Building Your Board: Proactive Values Minds Over Money

CERTIFICATE OF INCORPORATION

At the time a company is created, two key documents define the entity: the *articles of incorporation* and the *bylaws*, which we will refer to as the *operating agreement*. Following is a description of each of these documents:

> *Articles of incorporation.* When a new startup is established, the articles of incorporation are filed with the state government office in which the company is being created. Akin to a birth certificate, this document announces to the world that a company is born and announces its name, address, legal structure, and purpose. A registered agent, typically one of the founders or an attorney, signs this document and pays a modest fee to the secretary of state offices, receives an identification number, and the startup is formed.
>
> *Bylaws.* The bylaws of any company describe the decision-making processes, establish a chain of command, and define a governance structure. The various roles such as CEO, their process of election, and the responsibilities of each are defined. The board of directors is also identified, which at inception for most startups is usually made up of the founders.

The operating agreement of your company is like an operating system manual. At the minimum, every CEO should know the following:

> *Who makes the decisions?* Which decisions need more than just the CEO to decide? Specifically, when can a board make a decision or when is the consent of all, or a certain percentage of shareholders, required?
>
> *What is the decision-making process?* In the simplest case, the CEO makes the decision. But which decisions require a board or a shareholder vote? Who can propose a motion, how much and what kind of notice is required, and what percentage of the shareholders is required to approve a decision?
>
> *How do these decisions impact the business?* Most of the decisions that need to be approved by the board or shareholders will be significant decisions concerning the business. These are often a financing, a sale or IPO of the company, changing the capitalization structure, divesting assets, or replacing key members of the management team.

What if you disagree with the decision? The process for discussing the options and the rights of individual shareholders in the company if they disagree with the decision, while often limited, is spelled out in the operating agreement.

What you can do that will get you into legal trouble? This is code for "what should you be careful not to do," which, if you do it, will invalidate the decision and, in the most extreme case, might lead to your ending up in jail.

The following sample bylaws describe the formation of the board at the time of formation of the company:

Board: The business and affairs of the Company shall be managed by or under the direction of the Board.

Number of Directors: The Board shall consist of one or more members. The number of directors shall be determined from time to time by resolution of the Board.

Election, Qualification, and Term of Office of Directors: Directors shall be elected at each annual meeting of stockholders. Each director shall hold office until such director's successor is elected and qualified or until such director's earlier death, resignation, or removal.

THE IMPACT OF A FINANCING ON THE CERTIFICATE OF INCORPORATION

When the first round of capital is raised, the new investors and the company execute a *shareholder purchase agreement* (SPA) and *shareholder rights agreement* (SRA). The SPA defines the basics of the investment, while the SRA establishes the board structure and controls, including other duties of shareholders.

At the early stages, most venture capitalists (VCs) will seek oversight of and active participation in key decisions of the company. As part of this, they often require a seat on the board of directors. Even though an individual VC may have a minority ownership position in the company, the resulting board seat may have a disproportionately high influence on the decision making of a company. Boards that are one-sided can quickly become dysfunctional. Be careful not to end up in the position of the woeful entrepreneur who remarked, "My VC picked all the board members. I don't always see eye-to-eye with them. That has been a source of conflict, but we've learned to live with each other. At times, it has been tense."

During the financing process, the term sheet usually defines the size of the board and the parties represented by each board member. For example, a board may be composed of five members: two seats representing investors, two seats representing management, and one independent board seat. The term sheet can also describe the frequency of board meetings, formation of various board committees, and the process of any modification to the board structure on a going-forward basis.

Following is an example of language from a term sheet describing the board configuration and operating dynamics of the board.

Board of Directors

At the initial Closing, the Board shall consist of Five members comprised of:

   (i) [Name] as [the representative designated by [VC Fund] as the lead Investor,
  (ii) [Name] as the representative designated by the remaining Investors,
 (iii) [Name] as the representative designated by the Founders,
  (iv) the person then serving as the Chief Executive Officer of the Company, and
   (v) one person who is not employed by the Company and who is mutually acceptable to the Founders, Investors, and to the other directors.

Other Board Matters

Meetings: The Board of Directors shall meet at least quarterly, unless otherwise agreed by a vote of the majority of Directors.

Committee: Each Board Committee such as Audit and Compensation Committee shall include at least one Series A Director.

Number of Directors: The number of directors shall be determined from time to time by resolution of the Board.

Election, Qualification, and Term of Office of Directors: Directors shall be elected at each annual meeting of stockholders. Each director shall hold office until such director's successor is elected and qualified or until such director's earlier death, resignation or removal.

Often, in early-stage startups, one of the VCs is the lead investor and, as a result will heavily influence the board. These lead investors have the most money invested in the company and often have the largest ownership of the company. Even if they have the largest ownership position, they simultaneously have a duty as board members to represent the interests of all shareholders.[1] Thus, these lead investors have to act thoughtfully, which may at times conflict with their specific financial interests.

Management team members represented at the board level include founders and the CEO. When one of the founders is the CEO, there is obviously overlap in this seat. However, when the CEO is hired separately from the founders, the CEO almost always has a board seat.

These overlapping interests can create a set of complex dynamics. These can change after each new financing results in new investors, new voting thresholds, and new protective provisions. At a minimum, you should know the answers to the following questions:

Which decisions require board approval or shareholder approval? There are often different thresholds for each, and something that could be approved by just the board early on will now need to get shareholder consent later in the life of the company.

Which decisions require approval of preferred shareholders? Which require the approval of all shareholders? In some cases, the preferred shareholders will need to approve a decision. In others, a subset or threshold such as a majority or a super-majority is all that is needed. There may be multiple classes of preferred stock, each with a separate vote. And, finally, in some cases, approval of a majority of common shareholders will also be needed.

Can new directors be nominated or current directors be removed? If yes, what is the process? In some cases, you will want to add a new director or remove an existing director from the board. It's important to know the rules around this well before the situation arises.

WHY VCs WANT BOARD SEATS

While many VCs have been entrepreneurs, most entrepreneurs haven't been VCs. In order to understand why a VC wants a board seat as part of his investment, it's important to understand the motivation of a typical VC.

Before a VC can make investments, he and his firm have to raise a fund. VCs raise money from financial institutions, such as pension funds, foundations, family offices, and high-net-worth individuals, who are referred to as the limited partners, or LPs, in the fund. The performance expectation of the VC firm by the LPs is typically in excess of 20 percent annualized. The fundraising process can be long and arduous, taking as much as 18 months. Many a VC is humbled in this process and can empathize better with entrepreneurs when financial institutions do not return their calls, ask them to pitch their fund strategy in seven minutes, and offer no feedback or are unresponsive to the VC after the fundraising pitch.

Part of the promises VCs make to their LPs is active ownership and involvement in the companies the VC invests in. This is often called "VC value add," where the VC asserts that his involvement will help impact the outcome of the company in a positive way.

VC funds are closed-ended funds. Once the fund is raised, no new investors are admitted. The life of a VC fund is typically 10 years, with optional extensions (most early-stage VC funds actually last 12 to 15 years), and the expectation by the LPs that the VCs will exit their investments within this time frame. Each fund has an active investment period, typically 5 years, during which a VC firm can make investments in new companies. After the investment period is over, the fund can continue to make follow-on investments in existing companies that it has funded, but it can't invest in any new companies. As a result, most VC firms raise a new fund every 3 to 5 years so they are able to continue to make a steady stream of new investments. If a VC firm doesn't generate adequate returns for their investors, they can't raise a new fund and eventually have to close the firm.

Once a VC firm has raised a fund, they begin making investments. During this investment period, they actively search for companies to invest in, make the investments, and then manage the investments, which often includes taking a board seat. Over this investment period, a typical VC firm will make between 10 and 30 investments, depending on the size of the fund.[2]

Early in the life of a fund, a VC firm will typically generate negative returns as it is investing capital and taking management fees, but not generating any exits. This is called the "J Curve" (see Figure 5.2) and is a reason for the length of time it takes a fund to get into positive return territory.

In the first few years of the fund, VCs don't feel pressure to generate outcomes, as most LPs understand the J Curve dynamic. However, at some point, usually around the fourth or fifth year of the fund, there starts to be a series of forces that drive pressure for exits, including the desire of most

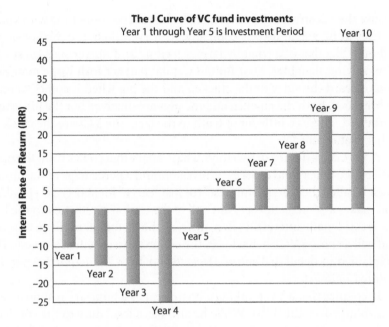

FIGURE 5.2 The J Curve of VC Investing

firms to raise another fund in that time period. As a result, some VCs start to pressure the companies they are investors in to sell earlier than the entrepreneurs might otherwise desire, or accept an offer at an intermediate stage from a buyer for a successful outcome, but at a price much lower than the entrepreneurs believe the company will be worth in a few years.

VC performance is measured two ways by LPs: cash-on-cash return and internal rate of return (IRR). Cash-on-cash return is an absolute measure that doesn't take into consideration the passage of time—it's simply the multiple of $ returned/$ invested. In contrast, IRR[3] is heavily time dependent—the faster a company is sold, the higher the IRR. A typical VC fund targets at least an IRR of 20 percent on an annualized basis. Given the time dependency of the IRR measure, there is pressure on the VC to have some exits earlier in the life of the fund.

While your VC may love you, she might love other companies in her portfolio more. When a VC invests, she believes she is investing in a potentially hugely successful company every time she makes an investment. However, in a typical VC fund, this only comes true 10 percent of the time or less. As a result, as you trend away from being a big success, your VC will take one of two paths. She will either start paying less attention to you because she doesn't see the upside, or she will spend more time with you as she tries to fix you and your company. And even then, the relationship is a bit odd, like that of a friendly farmer feeding and nurturing a turkey for Thanksgiving slaughter. First Round Capital partner Josh Kopelman says, "You've heard the story of the chicken and the pig when it comes to making breakfast. Both the chicken and the pigs are involved but the pig is fully committed. There's a little bit of truth to the fact. The VCs are the chickens in this relationship."

A VC makes money in two ways: a base salary that comes from the management fee that a fund charges its investors and a percentage of the profits, which is called the "carried interest" (or just "carry" for short). A typical VC fund makes a 20 percent carry after all of the capital is returned to the LPs. This creates many interesting dynamics, as the historical performance of a fund will impact a VC's behavior in the context of a specific company. This is explained in detail in *Venture Deals: Be Smarter Than Your Lawyer and Venture Capitalist*.

Recognize that a VC is taking a board seat as a fiduciary responsible to his own investors (his LPs). While he also has a legal duty to the company as a board member, his duty as a fiduciary to his investors will often take precedence. This can cause awkward issues at many points in a company's life. There are clear ways to resolve this but the tension often exists in the VC's mind, and is typically not explained or discussed when it is happening. Understanding what drives this conflict, how your VC thinks about it, and how he resolves it when it arises is important to get out in the open.

CHAPTER SIX

ALIGNING YOUR BOARD

Getting the right people on the board is a crucial first step. Making sure appropriate expectations are set and everyone is aligned on a common goal is equally vital.

"Your board is a disparate group of well-intentioned people who want to support you, be productive, and help the company be successful. But you need to invest the time and effort to understand each person and then bring all of it together and establish a common ground. It's like a subtle discovery process of each member's DNA," says Nexaweb Technologies CEO Chris Heidelberger.

You can achieve alignment of your board only if you understand your investors' motivation for making an investment, why they want to be involved with your board, how they think they can be additive to the mix, and their preferences for communication. "I would never invest in a company until I met each member of the board and made sure I understood how this board would behave, especially in rough times," says EDF Ventures co-founder Thomas Porter.

MOTIVATION AND COMMUNICATION

The reasons people invest in companies and join boards can vary considerably. As you explore motivations, start with the following questions:

Why did you invest in this company? This may seem like a trivial question, but you will be surprised how one board member's answer can differ from another. While most investors will have generic answers, such as "we believe in the founders" and "the market opportunity is enormous," look for answers that tell you how their experience, relationships, and deep domain insights allow them to understand the market opportunity and help build significant companies. Keep your eyes open for past investments in their portfolio that have grown rapidly. Understand how you fit into an investor's portfolio and how their existing portfolio can accelerate your own growth.

What are the top milestones you would like to see accomplished in the next 90 days? How about one year? The primary goal of this question is to ensure that all board members are aligned with these milestones. If you see wide variances in the answers, you know that you have misalignment to address up front. Steve Blank covers this topic very directly in his great book *The Startup Owner's Manual.* He begins early on with a checklist with 14 bullet points to ensure that you have alignment and agreement among investors, founders, and team. Some relevant points to consider include:

- Board buy-in for the customer discovery process.
- The number of funded pivots available—how often can you change course?
- Board agreement on funding needs for testing different markets.
- How the board will measure company progress?

What is your expectation of exit timing, path, and value? While many investors will have vague answers to this question, their answers will change over time based on the performance of the business. Establishing a baseline expectation shortly after the investment is made is important.

While the motivations of board members are an important starting point, it's also useful to understand how they think they can be helpful. Ask direct questions, such as "When it comes to helping startups, what are you most effective at doing?" or "How can you specifically help our company in the next year?" Don't be bashful about asking what the board member doesn't feel he is good at.

Good board members will be operationally distant—they will respect that they are supporting the CEO's efforts and not running the company. However, a good board can help establish best practices and improve operational execution. Blackberry vice president T. A. McCann comments, "One way to gauge the interest of a board member in some key operational tasks is to start with a soft volley—small, simple ways where you can test the dynamic. Some will jump in, some will defer, but this is an easy way to tease out their interest levels and decide whom to engage."

Understanding an individual board member's desired communication level and frequency is critical to establishing a board tempo. Rather than imposing a rhythm on your board members, ask them what they want and then try to accommodate them. Following are some key questions to address:

- What are your preferences on reporting?[1]
- What is your ideal board meeting content and format?
- Do you want to include the full management team in the board meeting?
- How often do you want in-person versus remote board meetings?
- Should we have an annual retreat of the entire board? Should the management team be included?
- Would you like to interact with advisory board members?
- Do you prefer a dinner with management before or after the board meeting?

While it is unlikely that you will have all your board members aligned on all of these questions, by asking up front you'll understand their preferences and desires. The art form of relationship management is to blend these answers into a meaningful set of processes to help keep everyone marching in the same direction. If you are struggling to get to a good place with this, ask your lead director for help.

COMPENSATION

Assuming you've managed to attract some awesome board members, how do they deserve to get paid? The answer is: it depends.

You should never pay a venture capitalist (VC) who sits on your board representing his investment. VCs are getting paid by their firms to make investments and sit on boards. This is their job. Most VCs have provisions in their agreements with their LPs that either expressly forbid payment or require the VC to remit any compensation they make as a board member back to their investors. VCs already have plenty of skin in the game since they have purchased equity in your firm—they don't need board compensation as well.

Occasionally, a VC will ask for additional compensation, usually a stock option grant for sitting on your board. If this is early in the life of your company, it should raise a red flag about the particular VC. If there was a specific agreement negotiated at the time of the investment, that's fine, but a request after the fact is inappropriate. The one exception is after a company has gone public, at which point some VCs will request a standard board options grant to continue serving on a public company board.

Outside board members are an entirely different matter, as it is expected that they will be compensated in some way. An option grant of the company's stock in the range of 0.25 to 1 percent of the company that vests from two to four years is the normal range. The absolute amount varies, and grants are larger earlier in the life of the company. One way to size the grant is to think of it as 25 to 50 percent of what you'd give to a VP-level hire.

Until your company is profitable you should never use cash as board member compensation. Board members should be willing to take stock and play for the upside. A board member who feels your cash is better off with them rather than invested in hiring another engineer or salesperson is probably not focused on the right things.

Like VCs, members of management who sit on the board should not be compensated specifically for their board service.

You should reimburse each board member for reasonable expenses incurred on your company's behalf, either for attending board meetings or for specific work done that was approved in advance. However, make sure that you have a direct conversation early on about what the definition of "reasonable" is. For some, this means Motel 6, and for others, this means the Ritz. For some it means flying coach; for others, it means buying a first-class ticket. Either way, don't let yourself be surprised after the fact.

ORIENTING YOUR NEW BOARD MEMBERS

When you add someone to your board, the CEO, along with one of the existing board members, should take the responsibility for orienting the new board member. New board members should be familiar with the legal structure and capitalization of the company, understand the current business model, and be up to speed on the status of the company.

While many companies handle this informally, a board orientation package is a good discipline for helping integrate a new board member. Think of this as what you would use to orient a new employee with a few extra items, including:

- Bios of current board members, observers, committees, and their contact information.

- Review of materials: board handbook, policies, past minutes.
- Board meeting schedule.
- Current board policies and practices, including committees, decision-making procedures, observer roles, liabilities and insurance coverage, indemnification, confidentiality, and conflict-of-interest policies.

LESSONS FROM EXPERIENCE

AWR Corporation CEO Dane Collins led his VC-backed company to a successful exit. An engineer by training, Dane joined AWR as vice president of engineering. Seven years after he joined AWR, he was appointed CEO. For nine years, Dane and his co-founders engaged with their seven-member board.

Five things I could have done differently to improve the quality of my board and end up with an even better outcome for the company:

1. *Construct the right board.* Any group of founders should start thinking about their board well before you raise your first round. There is no point getting a coach one day before the big game. We went after people we knew as opposed to the absolute best in class. If I were to do it again, I would certainly reach higher. In my opinion, people who understand startup challenges are much better board members than domain experts. Board dynamics are 95 percent social and 5 percent financial, so aim for the best.

2. *Have higher expectations.* We did not know what to expect from our board. Once I raised my expectations, thinking about getting help was productive. Any board can be tremendously helpful, but founders need to understand their strengths. Our board meetings were a series of exercises in spitting out facts. We never got out of the rut of status updates. If I were to do it again, I'd push for the strategic and minimize tactical.

3. *Know the motivations and limitations of your board.* Except for the best of them, a VC's primary contribution to a company is around financial transactions. VCs push for revenue growth, and some of them can become impatient—they wouldn't care if you sold hot dogs as long as you show growth year-over-year. A VC is also challenged on time and may not dig deep enough into your issues, as they may be spread too thin.

4. *Outside CEO challenges.* Like many VC boards, our board brought in a CEO. This individual was well connected in the industry but was a huge cultural mismatch. As a big company manager, he had not lived in the trenches, and the challenges of doing versus managing showed up quickly. Eventually, we parted ways and I stepped up in this role. Founders should not underestimate the insight they have into their own business—an outsider can rarely match this.

5. *The loneliness of a startup CEO.* In my personal growth, I had the CEO title for almost three years before I began to truly act like one. This quandary of the title versus practice was an internal struggle. An astute board member would have spotted that. Finally, my personal mentor was able to kick my butt and help me evolve into thinking, acting, and aiming higher.

Dane Collins, CEO, AWR Corporation

CHAPTER SEVEN

IS AN ADVISORY BOARD USEFUL?

Startups often attract industry luminaries as advisers and then showcase these individuals as members of an advisory board. An advisory board can help you navigate the tricky waters of an early-stage startup: attracting your first customer, developing your product, executing a financing, recruiting key people, and resolving issues with your co-founders. The guidance offered by an advisory board member may be similar to a formal board member, but there are some simple differences between the two.

While advisory board members provide coaching, industry insights, access to people who can be helpful to the business, and credibility, they do not have a responsibility to act in the interest of all shareholders. Specifically, an advisory board, unlike the board of directors, does not meet formally, have any control rights, or have typical director legal responsibilities such as "duty of care" and "duty of loyalty" (see Table 7.1). Rather than meeting as a group, many advisory board relationships are one-to-one with the CEO and happen as needed by the CEO. DFJ venture partner Heidi Roizen says, "Advisory boards themselves are useless—but the advisor role can be very valuable to the startup."

As entrepreneurs, you can choose your advisers but you may not necessarily always have the luxury to choose your board of directors. Greg Gottesman, managing director of Madrona Venture Group, says, "Startup CEOs often default to adding smart people on the board. But the default should be to be add them as a good advisory board member." As investors come in, they often request board seats, and this may call for replacing an existing board member. However, advisory board members are not necessarily impacted in such situations.

TABLE 7.1 How an Advisory Board Differs from a Formal Board

	Formal Board	Advisory Board
Appointed By	Investors and shareholders.	CEO and founders.
Engagement	Defined by term sheet and financing rounds. Regular board meetings and annual shareholder meeting.	Defined by CEO. As needed and lumpy. Often intense around certain key events.
Duties	Bound by formal duties of care and loyalty.	Bound by simple agreement.
Actions	Proactive and hands-on. Can fire the CEO.	Reactive and supportive.
Term	At least until the next financing round.	Can be permanent or fluid.
Responsibility	To all shareholders.	To the CEO or founder.
Interests	High. Financial, reputational, legal, and career risks.	Low. Little or no skin in the game.

SHOULD YOU HAVE AN ADVISORY BOARD?

Techstars a mentor-driven accelerator, often talks about "mentor whiplash"—the thing that happens when you get seemingly conflicting advice from multiple mentors. Talk to five mentors; get seven different opinions! This is normal since there is no correct or absolute answer in many cases. People have different perspectives and experiences, and they are responding to different inputs based on their own context, even if the data they are presented with look the same on the surface.

Recently, Steve Blank, consulting associate professor at Stanford, and Brad each put up articles on the WSJ Accelerators site (http://blogs.wsj.com/accelerators/). The question for the week was "When should you have a board of directors or a board of advisers?" Brad's answer was *Start Building Your Board Early*. Steve's was *Don't Give Away Your Board Seats*. On the surface they seem to be opposite views, but if you read them carefully, you'll see that they are saying similar things.

This is a classic case of mentor whiplash in the context of the question "When should you have a board of directors or a board of advisers?" Let's start with Steve's article.

I recently had a group of ex-students out to my home who were puzzling over a dilemma. They'd been working hard on their startup, were close to finding product/market fit, and had been approached by Oren, a potential angel investor. Oren had been investing since he left Google four years ago and was insisting on not only a board seat, but he wanted to be chairman of the board. The team wasn't sure what to do.

I listened for a while as they went back and forth on the matter. Then I asked: "Why should he even be on your board at all?" I got looks of confusion. Then they replied: "We thought all investors get a board seat. At least that's what Oren told us."

Uh-oh. Red flags just appeared in front of my eyes. I realized it was time for the board of directors versus advisers talk.

I pointed out that there are four roles a financial investor can take in your company: board member, board observer (a non-voting attendee of board meetings,) advisory board member, or no active role. I explained that as a non-public company, there was no legal requirement for any investor to have a board seat. Period. That said, professional venture capital firms that lead an investment round usually make their investment contingent on a board seat. And it sounded like, if successful, their startup was going to need additional funding past an angel round to scale.

In the past few years, it's become more common for angel investors to ask for a board seat, but I suggested they really want to think hard about whether that's something they need to do now.

Their reaction: "But how do we get the advice we need? We're getting to the point that we have lots of questions about strategic choices and relationships. Isn't that what a board is for? That's what we learned in business school."

I realized that while my students had been through the theory, it was time for some practice. So I told them: "At the end of the day, your board is not your friend. You may like them and they might like you, but they have a fiduciary duty to the shareholders, not the founders. And they have a fiduciary responsibility to their own limited partners. That means the board is your boss, and they have an obligation to optimize results for the company. You may be the ex-employees one day if they think you're holding the company back."

I let that sink it for a bit and then asked: How long have you worked with Oren?

I kind of expected the answer, but still was a bit disappointed. They said they met him twice, once over coffee and then over lunch.

I responded: "You want to think hard about appointing someone to be your boss just because they're going to write you what in the scheme of things will be a small check."

Now they looked really confused. They argued that they needed people with great advice who could help them with their next moves.

"Do you know what an advisory board is?" I asked. From the look on their faces, I realized they didn't, so I continued: "Advisers are just like they sound. They provide advice, introductions, investment, and visual theater—proof that you can attract A+ talent. An adviser that provides a combination of at least two of these is useful."

A "board" of advisers is not a formal legal entity like a board of directors. That means they can't fire you or have any control of your company. While some founders like to meet their advisers in quarterly advisory board meetings, most companies don't really have their advisory board meet as a group. You can connect with them on an "as needed" basis. While you traditionally compensate advisers by giving them stock, I suggest you ask them to match any grant with an equal investment in the company—so they have "skin in the game."

Equally important in an advisory board is a great farm team for potential outside board members. It allows you to work with them over an extended period of time and see the quality of their advice and how it's delivered. If they are world-class contributors, when you raise a Series A round and you need to bring in an outside board member, picking someone you've worked with on your advisory board is ideal.

Finally, I suggested that Oren's request to be chairman of a five-person startup seemed to be coming from someone looking to upgrade his or her resume, not to optimize their startup.

As we wrapped up, I offered that there was no "right answer" but they should think about their board strategy as a balance between the amount of control given to outsiders versus the great advice outsiders can bring. I suggested that if they could pull it off, they might want to consider keeping the board to the two founders for now, surrounded by great advisers, which may include their seed investors. Then when they get a Series A, they'll probably add one or two professional VCs on the board with one great adviser as an outside board member.

As my former students left my home, they started to go through the experienced executives they knew and who they were going to take out for coffee.

Steve Blank, Consulting Associate Professor, Stanford[1]

Now, let's see what Brad said in his blog.

Boards of directors play different roles at different points in a company's life. Early-stage boards of directors should be focused on being an extension of the team, helping the entrepreneurs get out of the gate, and getting the business up and running.

Often, entrepreneurs don't build a board until they are forced to by their VCs when they raise their first financing round. This is dumb, as you are missing the opportunity to add at least one person to the team who, as a board member, can help you navigate the early process of building your company and raising that first round. In some cases, this can be transformative.

While you'll often get advice to just have a "board of advisers" at the beginning, I've found that the formality of a board of directors is helpful to the entrepreneur by creating an additional level of commitment from the directors. It's easy to be an adviser—there's no formal commitment or legal responsibility to the company. However, if you are a director, then you suddenly have magical "fiduciary duties" that, while they rarely come into play early on, do increase the seriousness of the position.

Lots of entrepreneurs don't want to be hassled by a board of directors early on. The entrepreneurs want to control the company, don't want to be responsible to a board, or don't want to waste time communicating with board members. This is a classic error of thinking about the early-stage board incorrectly.

The job of a great early-stage board member is to reinforce the CEO and the entrepreneur's success. This can take many forms and styles, but fundamentally it's a support role, and the entrepreneurs now have another high-powered person on their team.

While you will eventually have investors on your board of directors, I encourage all entrepreneurs to add at least one outside director early in the life of the company. The best early stage directors are other CEOs, who can be peers to the founders and help them with things they don't understand, are struggling with, or are just missing. These CEOs should be more experienced or have different experiences, but they should also understand your domain and be willing to commit the time to helping you.

If you raise money from a VC early on, either in a seed or Series A round, expect the VC to want a board seat. If you have two VC investors, they'll each want a board seat. If you haven't focused on adding an outside director, now is the time.

A typical early-stage board configuration is two founders, two VCs, and one outside director. Try to keep balance between the number of founders and VCs on the board early on, with outside directors filling in the gaps.

Start the process early. View this as adding great talent to your team.

Brad Feld, Managing Director, Foundry Group,
http://blogs.wsj.com/accelerators/2013/06/17/brad-feld-start-building-your-board-early/

When you read Steve's article and hear, "Steve says don't add a board member until after you raise a VC round," and then read Brad's article and conclude, "Brad says add a board member before you raise a VC round," it's easy to say, "Wow—okay, that sort of—well—doesn't really help. I guess I have to pick sides." You can line up paragraphs and have an amusing "but Brad said, but Steve said" kind of thing.

But if you go one level deeper, they are both saying, "Be careful who you add to your board." An advisory board is a great way to "try before you buy."

ATTRIBUTES OF A USEFUL ADVISORY BOARD MEMBER

While some attributes of a useful advisory board member will overlap with a good board member, an advisory board is fundamentally different than a board of directors. The board of directors works for all shareholders, while the advisory board typically works only for the CEO. Following are some of the things a useful advisory board member will bring to the table:

Ability to complement the formal board member and investor skills and mind set. It's important that an advisory board member understand that he is playing a different role than a board member.

Long-term commitment. Creating a successful company takes a long time. While advisory board members can have short-term impact, they are much more effective if they have a long-term view to the development of the company.

Creative thinking. The CEO and members of the leadership team need as many creative inputs as they can get. While some of this can come from the board of directors, it's often limited by the dynamics between the board and a CEO. An advisory board member can be an important source of out-of-the-box thinking.

Responsiveness. Rapid response is critical—CEOs will be looking for specific help from advisory board members, and responses beyond a few days will be useless.

Emotionally stable and positive attitude. The CEO already has enough pressure from all areas of the business. The advisory board can be a safe, comfortable place for the CEO to explore specific issues and get direct advice and feedback.

Can invest some cash in the company and have skin in the game. Upfront Ventures partner Mark Suster writes in his blog, "Even getting $10,000 out of someone who's already a millionaire and super successful gets you emotional buy in. Therefore, you're more likely to get value."[2]

SELECTING ADVISORY BOARD MEMBERS

In his book *The Four Steps to Epiphany*, Steve Blank suggests that a startup should recruit five different kinds of advisory board members at various stages of a company's evolution.

1. Technical: Offers product development advice.
2. Business: Offers business strategy guidance.
3. Customer: Offers direction on product features/value proposition.
4. Industry: Brings domain expertise.
5. Sales: Counsels on sales tactics and demand creation.

Blackberry vice president T. A. McCann suggests that you start by identifying the skills you need to be successful as a business. Then list the skills of your founders and your board members. Use the information to determine where you have gaps, and add advisory board members who fill in those gaps.

In cases where your investors have little or no domain knowledge about certain aspects of your business, an advisory board can be a huge asset. Adam Rodnitzsky, ShopperTrak's director of product marketing, says, "We were engaging with the customers and knew much more about the space than anyone—the founders were the de-facto experts. But enterprise sales were our weakness. To address that, we got an adviser who knew all the challenges involved in the constellation of enterprise sales decision making. We had no appreciation for these challenges, but our adviser was a tremendous asset."

CHALLENGES OF ADVISORY BOARDS

While an advisory board can be helpful, it can also have dynamics that are dysfunctional, either at the specific adviser level or at the overall advisory board level. For starters, advisers might be excellent contributors as individuals, but not as a fully integrated functioning group. IronPort Systems co-founder Scott Bannister says, "At IronPort we had advisers, but not an advisory board. One adviser actually came to most board meetings despite having no seat, observer or otherwise. Another provided management and HR advice to the CEO. And we encouraged executives to have their own advisers as well. I think this works better than thinking of them as a board of any sort."

Advisory board members will have different levels of individual engagement. As founders, you have to define your expectations and make sure the advisory board member shares this. Many advisers sign up with immense enthusiasm only to vanish after the stock option agreements have been signed. Be clear on expectations, time commitments, and how you measure the advisory board members' contribution.

Make sure you understand any conflicts in advance. Great advisers will often be engaged with multiple startups. This can generate conflicts with regard to time, attention, or confidentiality. Advisers who function with high integrity will maintain confidentiality and respect your ideas, while others will be less careful. It's your duty to understand these conflicts before you sign up.

As a founder or CEO, you have many competing priorities. While having an advisory board may be useful, make sure you are committed to spending the time to cultivate and maintain the relationships. In the absence of your attention, the advisory board can turn into simply a list of names on your web site.

PART THREE

THE BUSINESS OF THE BOARD MEETING

CHAPTER EIGHT

THE ACTUAL BOARD MEETING

"You have received their investment—now stop selling, please," says Cooley LLP partner Eric Jensen. "CEOs often start their first board meeting as if they are making an investor pitch—sharing how great their company is, how big the market is, and describing the vision, which is no longer necessary. The investors are now in the boat and it's time to start rowing with their help."

A typical board meeting runs from one to four hours, depending on the agenda. The meeting starts with the chair calling the meeting to order followed by the CEO providing an update on the business and a summary of key metrics. The chief financial officer (CFO) provides a financial update. The VP of sales walks through the previous quarter's performance and upcoming quarter's pipeline. The VP of engineering demonstrates key features in the next release, and the VP of marketing reviews the launch plans. After the updates, the board tackles substantive issues, typically covering one to three big issues. The board is interactive, asking questions and providing guidance and real-time feedback during the discussion. Finally, at the end of the meeting, the CEO steps out, and the board conducts a brief executive session to discuss the progress and any concerns that have arisen. The chair then follows up with the CEO to discuss anything that came up in the closed session.

"The art of a good board meeting requires the CEO to bring out the critical issues, stimulate a productive discussion in a non-threatening fashion, and get consensus in a timely manner," says EDF Ventures co-founder Thomas Porter.

CREATING AN ANNUAL CALENDAR

Regardless of the frequency of your board meetings, create an annual calendar at the beginning of the year. While it might seem tedious to try to schedule things for an entire year, recognize that your board members, especially your investors who may serve on a dozen boards, have extremely busy calendars.

The frequency of meetings varies based on the stage of a company, but at the minimum you should have one meeting a quarter. "Most startups have meetings much more frequently, sometimes as often as once a month. Things change so quickly, and investors also don't understand your business well enough in the beginning. In two months, a lot can change in a pure startup."[1] Upfront Ventures partner Mark Suster suggests a monthly rhythm for the first two years, followed by every six weeks in years three and four, and then bimonthly or quarterly thereafter.

THE MEETING AGENDA

Develop and publish the meeting agenda in advance of the meeting. Orbotix CEO Paul Berberian encourages using the agenda to bring focus to the key issues. "Prior to any board meeting, I simply ask myself, what is the one sentence I want them to hear at this meeting—is it all systems go? We are on target—or do we need help? I try to summarize the meeting in three minutes and then build it up from there."

A good board meeting addresses the most critical issues first and focuses on strategic issues facing the business. The business updates should be covered in advance of the meeting in the board package. The review of the business should take at most 30 minutes of the actual meeting, as the bulk of the meeting should be focused on strategic issues.

Many startup CEOs front-load the agenda with updates and push the strategy discussion items to the end of the meeting. There is no focus on the key issues, the meeting drifts because there is no tight agenda, and before you know it, board members have to rush to catch their flights. In this type of a board meeting, the most important agenda items do not get adequate attention. This is a recurring flaw most board members see and complain about. In a McKinsey study of 586 corporate directors, respondents pointed out that they would like to double their time on strategy discussions.[2]

The CEO is responsible for setting the agenda for each meeting, but should use the lead director to help surface and vet the key issues in advance of the meeting. Nexaweb Technologies, CEO Chris Heidelberger talks about what he has learned over time about setting the actual board meeting agenda.

> I was not well prepared to manage the board the first time around. A CEO's job is to lead the board—I was less prepared and comfortable in setting the tone and being the leader in the context of majority shareholders. It changed very quickly—my role is to lead vigorously.
>
> I was going to the board to seek advice and input on strategy and direction. I led the agenda with several open-ended questions.
>
> The more appropriate way is to set the direction and then invite feedback. Process that feedback and decide what's valuable and what's not. Eventually, show what advice you have incorporated.
>
> The biggest mistake I made was going into board meetings with big open-ended questions. It's not necessarily a group of advisers.
>
> *Chris Heidelberger, CEO, Nexaweb*

FOCUS ON CRITICAL ITEMS

Rather than get caught up in the day-to-day details of the business, try to use your board to help you address key strategic challenges. Is your business model changing? Do you have a key partnership that can make or break the business? When do you need a new round of financing? Do you have a key executive who isn't cutting it?

Conflicts between management team members, specific board members, or between management and the board are particularly important to address. "In such situations, be open and honest—don't try to game the board," says Thomas Porter. "They will see it instantly." As CEO, you will be more effective if you master the basis of conflict. In the book *Crucial Conversations: Tools for Talking When Stakes Are High*,[3] the authors offer a set of tools that anyone can use to handle conflict in an adult manner, which include:

- *Commit to seek mutual purpose.* We all want this company to be successful.
- *Recognize the purpose behind their strategy.* You are not satisfied with this situation or outcome and wish to do something about it. I understand your position.

- *Invent a mutual purpose.* When we get past this situation our company can be stronger.
- *Brainstorm new strategies.* How about we focus on cost cutting and reducing our cash burn for now instead of raising another round down the road?

Renaissance Venture Capital CEO Christopher Rizik suggests an approach for framing these discussions at a board level. "First of all, as CEO, the board has invested in you. Do not make the board work more than you need to—develop a framework and offer some options along with a recommendation."

Rally Software CEO Tim Miller states, "If you are uncertain on how to approach a problem, start one-on-one with a key board member." Rather than making a bunch of assertions or asking open-ended questions, frame the issues as hypotheses using language like:

- Here is a problem and I don't know the answer—give me some insights on where to start.
- Here is what I want to do—tell me if I am wrong.
- I have made this decision and I want to get your views.

VictorOps CEO Todd Vernon talks about how important it is to do your homework and analysis in advance of asking the board a question.

I think you can ask any question of your board that you want to, but the price of entry is you have to do some homework—show them your analysis. You have to provide them the data to give you the answer. Show them your best analysis and how you've weighted it. Then ask the question.

Young CEOs don't do this because they're afraid that they're going to provide two analyses of a situation, and the obvious one was a third that they didn't even think of. But that's the price of entry—such challenges come with the territory of being around smart Type A people. I would never ask a question in a meeting without having my own version of the answer prepared and somewhat thrown out on the table. The worst thing that can happen is they'll all have a different opinion of what you should do. And they're not going to agree. But worse, they will think: Why is he asking us—it's his company? It's one of the biggest faux pas you can do as a CEO.

Todd Vernon, CEO, VictorOps

SENDING OUT THE BOARD PACKAGE

You should send the board package out at least 48 hours in advance of the meeting. Give your board members enough time to read the board materials.

Trada CEO Niel Robertson offers a view on the negative cycle of meaningless board meetings that results from the last-minute rush.

> For the most part CEOs don't communicate on a regular basis with board members. They view the board meetings as a time where they communicate with the board. So they put together a board packet and they send it off a few hours in advance or the night before. This is the one of the worst behaviors of CEOs. And the board member shows up, they haven't had time to digest that board packet; and so they're learning all the developments in real time. It forces them to serve up platitudes, leading to trite and banal remarks. You want them to be actually quite contextual, very specific. By not giving them enough time to process the materials, you have lost that opportunity.
>
> *Niel Robertson, CEO, Trada*

Madrona Venture Group strategic director William Ruckelshaus says, "A board member often doesn't think deeply about the company until he starts preparing for the meeting. To get good perspective, the CEO has to share good information ahead of time so that the board member can be prepared."

When board members have not reviewed the materials in advance, very little substantive or useful conversation follows. Niel Robertson states:

> The board feels like they have to add value, they have to say something. In such a situation, 95% of the discussion is basic business and the 5% critical issues get postponed because no one has any real inputs. This is a very negative cycle that continues since the board doesn't really know what is going on. As a result, the CEO essentially is just trying to figure everything out alone. This creates a really horrible board dynamic that eventually blows up.

MEETING LENGTH

A typical board meeting lasts from one to four hours. It's the lead director's and the CEO's responsibility to ensure that the meeting begins and ends on time. Having a social experience, either dinner the night before or after the board meeting, often helps create a more substantive relationship among board members.

Return Path CEO Matt Blumberg talks about the value of socializing the board:

A high-functioning board isn't materially different from any other high-functioning team. The group needs to have a clear charter or set of responsibilities, clear lines of communication, and open dialog. And as with any team, making sure that the people on a board know how to connect with each other as individuals as it's critical to building good relationships and having good communication, both inside and outside of board meetings. We've always done a dinner either before or after every in-person board meeting to drive this behavior. They take different forms: sometimes they are board only, sometimes board and senior management; sometimes just dinner, sometimes an event as well as dinner, like bowling (the lowest common denominator of sporting activities) or a cooking class. But whatever form the "social time" takes, and it doesn't have to be expensive at all, I've found it to be an incredibly valuable part of team building for the board over the years. You'd never go a whole year without having a team dinner or outing . . . treat your board the same way!"

Matt Blumberg, CEO, Return Path,
http://www.onlyonceblog.com/2007/11/the-social-aspe

A BOARD CALL INSTEAD OF A MEETING

Often, board calls happen on short notice. These generally are done via a conference call instead of a physical meeting. Occasionally, the board meeting is merely a periodic update and a call will suffice. In these situations, information flows mostly one way—from the CEO to the board. If there are specific items to discuss or vote on, they should be well framed by the CEO or the lead director. Recognize that any topic that requires a deep discussion, deliberation, or meaningful engagement is better suited for a face-to-face board meeting.

While speed and efficiency are the obvious advantages of a call, the challenges include dropped calls, lack of engagement, or rapport. Building consensus via a phone call also has its own challenges, especially around complex topics. As a result, for a call, have a tight agenda, a clear leader on the call, and written material distributed ahead of time.

If you choose to make a formal motion via a call, start with a roll call of attendees. Participants should have an opportunity to weigh in and assert their position. Ask each one formally to speak, especially those who may be silent: "Jack, we have not heard your opinion on this. Could you share your thoughts?" If one person dominates the conversation, try saying, "Thank you for your opinion. Can we also get the others to weigh in?" Clarify each person's position with a statement such as "So before we wrap up, let me make sure I've gotten all of your feedback."

REMOTE ATTENDEES

When you have one or more remote attendees at a board meeting, consider using a videoconference instead of an audio conference. Low-end video-conferencing, via Skype and Google Hangouts, is often completely adequate these days. Higher-end dedicated videoconferencing systems, such as Cisco and Lifesize, are also affordable.

Videoconferencing changes the dynamics dramatically. If done correctly, it's just marginally less effective than having the person in the room. Unlike an audio conference, where people can easily drift away, check their e-mail, or be passively engaged, it's harder to hide when you are in a videoconfer-ence. And it's correspondingly harder for the people in the room to forget about the remote attendees.

Videoconferencing, especially on low-end services, functions using the least common denominator rules—the weakest connection will determine the quality of the call. If you are having connectivity issues on a videoconfer-ence, especially if audio is weak, shift the audio to a separate channel from the video by using a separate conference call for everyone to dial into for audio. Then, mute everyone on the videoconference side and just use the videoconference for video.

Over the past few years, we've increasingly used videoconferencing for remote attendance at meetings. When done right, it's remarkably effective and almost as good as being there.

MEETING HYGIENE

As the CEO, it's your meeting—you get to define the meeting hygiene. Articulate this clearly, simple things like whether phones are permitted to be on in the meeting or whether people can check their e-mail during the meeting. Do you have a culture of laptops in the meeting, or should all computers, tablets, and smartphones be put away? Do you have a five-minute break every hour or should people just get up and go to the bathroom when they need to?

Food is another meeting hygiene issue that is often overlooked. Brad is a vegetarian and has been at thousands of board meetings where his only choice for something to eat was a ham sandwich and potato chips. You don't have to be extravagant, especially if you are a pre-revenue startup, but knowing your board members' individual food and drink preferences and putting a little effort into accommodating them sets a positive tone.

While it may seem trivial, if everyone knows about and operates using the same ground rules, you'll have a much more effective meeting. Mutual respect will be higher as no one will be observing a different cultural norm in the meeting that will cause others to feel disrespected.

MANAGING INTERPERSONAL DYNAMICS

Board relationship management and the underlying dynamics require continual attention. Niel Robertson states, "I don't decouple the concepts of a board meeting from the board relationship—the two are very neatly tied together. If you have a weak relationship with your individual board members, the board meeting structure changes pretty dramatically. If you have a much closer and consistent relationship with your board, the board meeting dynamics are much different."

As the leader of the company, the CEO should set expectations around how decisions will get made. Techstars Managing Director Mark Solon explains, "It's really important for the CEO to lay out the dynamic in the first board meeting. It could be as simple as saying, 'I will seek your advice but I'll make the decisions. If you're unhappy with my performance, you can fire me.' It's important for a first-time entrepreneur who is surrounded by more experienced investors to not get bullied into their telling him how to run his business." This is not about being in charge; rather, it's about setting the tone and culture of leading the board.

Some personalities are stronger than others, and it's likely you'll face the challenge of overbearing board members. Upfront Ventures partner Mark Suster writes:

> Board meetings often end up being a debate between the CEO and the board member who likes to hear himself speak the most. You probably have lots of great ideas around the table—but the same people speak over and over again. The best way to stop this, as a CEO is (a) don't let yourself be the "chalk and talk" type who wants to drive through all your key points at the board meeting, and (b) whenever you bring up a topic for discussion (as in the strategic topics) make sure to call on everybody. When the "talker" keeps jumping in, politely say, "That's great. I appreciate your input." Write down what they said on a white board (so they feel listened to) but then go around the room and call on everybody, "So what do you think?"[4]

Jacques Benkoski, a partner at US Venture Partners, recalls a first-time CEO who was gifted in running board meetings. "Here was a young man in his late twenties—when any Type A board member would try to derail the flow of the meeting, he would calmly say, 'Good point. Why don't we address this as soon as we make a decision on this current agenda item?' Sometimes, when Type A's dominate the conversation and fill it up with noise, the wise ones will stay silent. You risk losing their insights if you do not draw out their opinions. You don't have to try and wring out anything from anyone—at times, people don't have a point of view. But try to get a perspective from your most experienced board member."

Todd Vernon warns:

> There's always one dude in the room who sucks all the air out of it. And it can easily just devolve into a meeting with one person because all the others will just sit there and watch. Soon, they're not talking about the company anymore at all. They're trying to prove something to each other. It's a funny dynamic and the most important thing a CEO can do is to figure out how to make decisions while ensuring they all get along. Or remove situations where you know they're not going to get along—you have to keep the meeting on track.

Renaissance Venture Capital CEO Christopher Rizik suggests that an easy way to minimize such a dynamic is to work closely with the chair. "When one board member tends to pull the meeting in his direction consistently, it's a delicate position for a CEO to be in. And they should not hesitate to ask the chair for help—a good chair helps keep the meeting on track." Eric Jensen adds, "CEOs unknowingly create a board dynamic which can lead to micromanagement. I always ask the CEO, 'What did you do to create such a situation?' In some cases, VCs drive this behavior. The chair should be cognizant of it and act as a shield if needed."

Andreessen Horowitz partner Scott Weiss says:

> Private company information is asymmetrical, and so there's definitely a lot of power jockeying around—typically the people that have the most information occasionally like to stretch their muscles. They say things like "you didn't hear this from me but . . ." and then go on to share confidential details. If such a guy is on my board and he was sharing this at other board meetings, I would not be happy. I've seen this kind of behavior and I like to slap it whenever I see it.

As CEO, it's your responsibility to relentlessly guard the culture of the boardroom. Focus on the solution, minimize ego and hyperemotional dramas, and avoid blame and emotional poison, including politics, gossip, and backstabbing. Watch for those who thrive in such environments and call them out before the poison spreads.

INCLUDING YOUR TEAM IN THE BOARD MEETING

There's a lot of value in including your entire team in the board meeting. However, while this is your opportunity to sit back and let your team shine, it is not a social feel-good event. Rather than feel like you need to have each member of the team take an active role in the meeting, let the agenda drive the engagement. Avoid filling the boardroom with too many bodies, as it can devolve into a counterproductive parade.

Niel Robertson has flipped this dynamic on its head and formulated a no-firewall policy:

> Any of my board members can come to any meeting. And some of them come to a lot of our company meetings. They'll come and sit in our executive staff meetings. I set up a no firewall rule with my board. Anybody can say anything, people can send him

e-mails—they don't have to ask me, they don't have to copy me on it. I've been in many companies where the CEO gets worried. You do not talk to board members unless you talk to me first. No firewall policy is not for all CEOs nor for all boards—this can be a gut checking, hard to swallow, stomach-turning experience for the CEO but if the board expects it, just do it.

THE EXECUTIVE SESSION

Board meetings should always end with an executive session. We recommend a three-step process. First, there should be an executive session with all board members. Anyone not on the board (observers and management team members) should leave. This gives the board a chance to have a "closed board meeting" that also has the benefit of being attorney-client privileged[5] in case any sensitive information needs to be discussed.

At the end of the full-board executive session, there should be a second executive session with non-management board members. In this session, the CEO and any other management team member who is on the board leaves. The remaining board members discuss any fundamental concerns they have about the CEO, the direction, or the dynamic of the company. The lead director should facilitate this session and summarize the discussion at the end.

The final step in the process is for the lead director to meet privately with the CEO and discuss any issues that came up in the second session. This feedback should be precise—the lead director should be careful not to editorialize.

In most cases the executive session will be a nonevent, especially if the culture of the board is to be open and direct. However, if there are leadership issues or fundamental concerns about the company or the CEO, the executive session creates a relatively safe environment to bring these issues up. By having a separate executive session after every board meeting, the awkwardness of calling a separate session is avoided, as there is an opportunity at every board meeting to have this type of discussion.

Jeff Bussgang, general partner at Flybridge Capital Partners, writes:

When I was an entrepreneur, I was initially uncomfortable with this idea of stepping out of the room so that the board could talk about me and "my company." But I came to appreciate the value of the private session for both the board and the company. It's an opportunity for the board to gain alignment on the key takeaways, direction to give the management team, and a forum to make decisions around compensation and bonuses, CEO performance feedback, financing, and generally build a functional decision-making unit.[6]

AFTER THE MEETING

A board meeting is always a learning experience of processes, personalities, and group dynamics. Graphicly CEO Micah Baldwin warns, "How you run a meeting is an indication of how you run the company—if the meetings start late, materials are sloppy or not on time, you are bouncing around all over the place . . . the VCs will think, 'Hmmm . . . is this how you run your company as well?'"

Board members can quickly become frustrated when critical issues such as a low cash position, poor market adoption, or endless changes in strategy are ignored. If the CEO does not raise issues directly, a good board will bring those up. EDF Ventures co-founder Thomas Porter says, "If you don't ask for help, especially in challenging times, the board will step in and offer help—and then eventually ask you to step aside." Tim Miller adds, "As an early-stage CEO, you need to develop the confidence to admit that you don't know. Only then you will get help."

Good boards appreciate the fact that CEOs listen and follow up with feedback or clarifications. If you call a board member after the board meeting with a simple question such as, "I wanted to make sure I did not miss your point. Did you mean . . . ," that speaks to your ability to understand what was said.

When BigDoor chief technical officer Jeff Malek reflected on a difficult board meeting, he realized he was worried about a few points that board members brought up. The word *casual* came up a few times in the meeting and Jeff was concerned. He went back, reflected on the situation, and then wrote an e-mail to make sure he did not stay "casual." Brad responded with a public blog post (with Jeff's permission), which follows (see p. 99).

I have a retrospective addiction. But as a result of looking back at our meeting today, Brad, words like *casual* still ringing in my ears, I recognized I'd let some of my own assumptions drive away potential opportunities, maybe even creating some problems along the way. I've always run under the assumptions that:

- Your inbox is an order of magnitude more onerous than mine (quite).
- The best way to respect and value your time would be to limit e-mail/communication.
- You and Keith have regular communications complete with bits about what I'm up to and thinking.
- You know even in the absence of communication from me that I'm working like a madman, doing everything I can to make it happen.
- You also know through some process of osmosis how much I value you, Foundry, your approach, feedback, etc.

Just so you don't get the wrong idea, it's not that I took your feedback and concluded that I needed to give you more BigDoor insight, or that you needed more info in general to get a better picture—that's what the numbers are for.

So while all of the above assumptions are probably true to some degree, here's the new protocol I'm going to start optimistically running under:

- Thanks to your candor and aversion to BS, you'll tell me to STFU as needed.
- You'd like a concise ping about whatever, whenever from me.
- You'll give me feedback if/when it makes sense to, and I won't expect a reply otherwise, unless I'm asking a direct question.
- Doing so is likely to benefit both of us, one way or another—hopefully more candid feedback will ensue.
- You know that I value your time highly, and mine specifically in the context of devoting most waking hours to making BigDoor a success.
- You know that I am incredibly grateful to know you and have you as an investor.

Those are my new assumptions. I felt like giving this topic some time and thought, glad I did, will keep it (mostly) short going forward but hopefully you know a bit more about where I'm coming from, out of this.

Thanks again for the time today, I thought it was an awesome f-ing meeting. I always leave them on fire.

Jeff Malek, CTO, BigDoor,
www.feld.com/wp/archives/2012/02/retrospective-addiction-of-a-
madman-post-board-meeting.html

A board member can play a meaningful role to ensure clarity and follow-up. Greg Gottesman, managing director of Madrona Venture Group, states:

> Often, I'll go back to the CEO after the board meeting and say something along the lines of "We talked about our market entry plan. Just so there's no confusion, here's where we came out on that." Or I say, "At this board meeting, we spent a little bit too much time on information and not enough time on some of the key strategic issues. Let's just focus the next meeting on this one strategic issue."

If a board member suggests an action item, which may be searching for a simple data point or conducting an extensive evaluation, address the request. Ensure that the request is aligned with current needs of the business, is not too arbitrary, and is actionable. Before you commit resources, make sure that other board members are aligned with the request. For example, a board member might suggest an irrelevant business action such as "Let's create a model to assess the impact of a meteor hitting the earth." Rather than ignore it, address it with whoever requested it, calibrating the value of the request with other board members, and explicitly decide whether to do it.

Board meetings help a CEO build focus and discipline in their own world. Todd Vernon says:

> The board meeting theoretically is for you; it's not for the board member. It helps you to keep track of where you are going. It is really important that a CEO gets in the discipline of developing strong metrics, measuring these regularly and sharing these with an outside party in an objective manner. Two years down the road, that discipline, including the metrics and reports, will be extremely valuable when those new investors come in.

Don't ever get complacent about the board meeting. Paul Berberian points out, "The first board meeting is easy—almost a gimme—it's the romantic phase. It's the eighth board meeting that I worry about; I want to make sure complacency does not set in. I have to be well prepared—every time you are in front of the board, it's an opportunity for them to judge you."

CHAPTER NINE

MOTIONS AND VOTES

While a startup may not need a highly formal board meeting, there are still some formal aspects of the meeting that should be incorporated and followed. These include:

- *Notice of meeting.* Providing the board members advance notice of the meeting. This is especially important for any votes that require shareholders to make.
- *Quorum.* Ensure that you have a quorum of the board. While this is often a majority, there are cases where the number of board members that constitute a quorum is defined in the organizing documents.
- *Agenda.* The agenda for the topics that are going to be covered in the board meeting.
- *Record keeping.* Minutes from the meeting should be taken, including a formal record of any motions, votes, and approvals.

ROBERT'S RULES OF ORDER

Board meetings are governed by a parliamentary procedure called Robert's Rules of Order.[1] Authored and published by Brigadier General Henry Martyn Robert in 1876, these rules have largely stayed the same over the years. Ironically, Robert wrote the manual in response to his poor performance in leading a church meeting and resolved that he would learn about parliamentary procedure before attending another meeting.

Robert's Rules of Order are a set of rules for conduct at meetings that allow everyone to be heard and to make decisions without confusion. This approach is a time-tested method of conducting formal business at board meetings and can easily be adapted to fit the style and needs of the company.

Organizations using Robert's Rules of Order typically have a short formal section at the beginning of the meeting, where the meeting is called to order by the chair, a quorum is confirmed, minutes from the prior meeting are approved, and any specific motions and votes are made for recurring actions such as stock option grants.

THE AGENDA

A board meeting can be a regular update meeting or a special meeting to discuss certain developments. In either case, the agenda should be defined and published in advance. Following are some examples of agenda items:

Officer reports. This is primarily when the CEO and his or her team presents the business updates, discuss strategy, finance, and relevant business matters.

Key business decisions. When you anticipate a shift in business model, new markets, hiring or firing key team members, or raising a round of financing, discuss it first with your board. The essence of this is simple: the investors agreed to a plan, and if you change the plan substantially, it's your duty to get inputs from the board.

Management. The board typically approves key management hires and their compensation. As the direction of the company depends on its key hires, your board often wants to be involved in—and can provide significant help with—key hiring decisions.

Equity-related decisions. All governance and control aspects in any financing are designed to protect the ownership interests of investors. The business value can be impacted due to internal performance issues (poor performance leads to cash challenges or lower valuation) or external financings (down rounds, debt obligations). Investors will often create special voting rights (over and above those of the board) to exercise control over key aspects of the company.

Raising new rounds of capital. Any new financing impacts the ownership of the company. Existing investors and board members typically approve the next financing—pricing of stock, the amount being raised, and the type of investors.

Stock option grants. Establishing an option pool may require shareholder approval, as it has a dilutive impact on all shareholders. If an option pool is already in place, the board approves granting options to key executives via a formal vote.

Annual budgets. Annual budgets are directly related to the key milestones of the company and spend rates. The board typically approves an annual plan and all major budget items.

Debt obligations. Any secured debt creates a lien on assets of a company and can be a drain on cash. Under the right circumstances, debt is additive to a company's capital structure. The board should be involved in any debt discussions and approvals.

Acquisition activity. Board members are heavily involved in all merger and acquisition activity, as they represent all shareholders and should be informed and express an opinion at all steps along the way to a deal.

Committee reports. Each formal committee, such as comp, audit, or nominating, should have time for specific discussion on any active issues from each committee.

Announcements and adjournment. It's customary to align calendars for the next meeting or remind members of the following meeting date, time, and venue.

HAVE YOUR LAWYER AT THE MEETING

Make sure that your company's attorney or outside counsel comes to the board meetings. In addition to recording the minutes, he can advise the board on any specific issues, remind everyone of the requirements on different voting matters (e.g., can the board approve something or is a shareholder vote required?), and creates a situation where the discussion at the board meeting is attorney-client privileged.[2] In addition, a good outside counsel is also a business adviser, and having him in the loop on what is going on enables him to provide better advice.

Most lawyers will offer a low, or even free, rate for attending board meetings, especially for early-stage companies. As Cooley LLP partner Eric Jensen says, "Good CEOs do not focus on legal fees; rather, make sure the procedures are followed correctly and records are maintained accurately." The board meeting minutes, votes, and records often create a platform of transparency and governance on which the follow-on investors lay their trust and confidence.

THE MECHANICS OF VOTING ON MOTIONS

Board members can present motions or request them to be put on the agenda. These motions are proposals for the entire board to act upon. The bylaws of a company define how motions are presented and decided upon, so make sure you understand how this works for the board you are on.

Technically, early-stage companies will seldom have much protocol and fanfare, and it is unlikely that an elaborate parliamentary procedure will be followed. However, formal board meetings are conducted to approve and record key action items, especially those that affect all shareholders. Therefore, it is essential for any entrepreneur to understand the procedure by which a motion is proposed, voted on, adopted, or debated.

The procedure for making a motion and seconding it, followed by approval of the chair, is as follows:

"Chair, I move that we approve the proposed business budget and plan for forthcoming annual year."

After a motion is made, another board member should second the motion, quite simply by saying "Second." If another member does not second the motion, the chair can call for a second. Note that, technically, if there is no second to the motion, the motion is lost. If there is a second, the chair will restate the motion. *"It has been moved and seconded that the budget and plan for forthcoming year has been adopted without changes"*; thus, the chair places your motion before the board for consideration and action. The board then either debates the motion or moves directly to a vote.

Motions will be presented, debated, and voted on in no particular order. Whoever makes the motion should speak first. The chair should moderate the discussion.

After the motion has been debated, the chair asks, "Are you ready to vote on the motion?" If there is no more discussion, a vote is taken. A chair may ask, "All in favor?," and those who agree to the motion will say "Aye." Most startup board votes are unanimous, but for protocol, the chair will follow this question with "Any opposed?," which is to record the "Nays."

Assuming that the motion has majority votes (or unanimous votes, as governed by the bylaws), the chair says, "If there is no objection or discussion, motion is approved." The secretary of the company will record these motions and votes for the minutes of the meeting, which are generally approved at the start of the next board meeting.

Two other motions that relate to voting are:

Motion to table. This motion is often used in the attempt to kill a motion.

Motion to postpone. While this is unlikely to occur in venture-backed companies, it is often used as a means of parliamentary strategy and allows opponents of a motion to test their strength without an actual vote's being taken.

The secretary records the minutes of any board meeting. Generally, minutes are brief, factual statements that state the resolutions and outcomes. Board books, minutes, and resolutions are available for reference in legal and acquisition-related discussions. It is important to maintain accuracy and timeliness of these corporate records since they are a layer of formal documentation around the company.

WHAT IF YOU DO NOT AGREE TO A MOTION?

Conflict and disagreement can arise between various board members, especially investors and management. The best approach to this conflict is to try to address and resolve it outside the context of a board meeting, but this isn't always possible.

Occasionally, the board will make a decision outside the context of a board meeting. This is often the case around a financing or change in leadership, especially concerning the CEO. In these cases, while it may feel like there is uniform agreement on a course of action, there may be differing views or changes in perspective as the decision is discussed further. While some board members are dogmatic, feeling that once a decision is made it should be executed on regardless of the feedback, we've found that continuous, open, and constructive discussion, especially when there is uncertainty or points of difference, is a powerful way to work though the issue at hand.

In early-stage boards, if you get to a point of a serious conflict, make sure you know who is going to support an issue well in advance of any formal activity. Then, approach the situations where there are disagreements with real formality, following the appropriate procedures. Resolve the issue, make your decisions, and try to move past the conflict.

DEALING WITH FORMAL ITEMS

Given that there will always be some formal activity at any board meeting, address the formal items up front, especially any matters that require votes. This is contrary to the flow of many startup company board meetings, where the CEO uses the meeting to set issues up and then crams in a bunch of formal decisions at the end when everyone is running out of time.

Several years ago, Brad tried turning the agenda on all of his board meetings upside down. The formal stuff went first. Everything else followed. The result was a much more engaged and informed board meeting. If there were formal items that required discussion, they were dealt with at the beginning of the meeting when everyone was fresh and alert. If formal discussions needed more time or more information, that became clear quickly and the appropriate time was allocated to them.

This was in stark contrast to trying to deal with the formal items at the end, which served to cut short the rest of the meeting while giving short shrift to the formal items. In addition, as the clock ran out on the meeting, board members would flee to whatever they needed to do next.

While the formal items typically don't require a lot of discussion, they occasionally do, and there seems to be a high correlation between having important voting items left and having no time left to talk about them. By addressing the formal issues at the beginning of the meeting and giving everyone enough time to address them, the balance of the meeting is free to follow whatever tangents it wants, without the anxiety building about running out of time to get to the formal items.

When it comes to approving major decisions, Upfront Ventures partner Mark Suster points out:

> Nothing major is ever decided at the board meeting. All super important issues should be lobbied and agreed before board meetings. You should know what each individual's view is and make sure you can count on their vote. I always like to tell people that if there's an important discussion at today's meeting and you're not "in on" what the decision is, you're the sucker in the room.[3]

MINUTES

At any board meeting, minutes need to be written that generally describe the topics discussed. By law, one needs to create minutes to prove there was a legally held board meeting. The board minutes show that the board is complying with all of its legal duties.

Some of the topics brought up in the meeting—especially voting issues—need to be recorded in detail. For instance, if the board votes to issue options to employees, take on a new round of financing, settle litigation, or sell the company, these actions and the corresponding motions and resolutions should be carefully detailed and accurately recorded. Usually, in these cases, you'll want your lawyer to draft the minutes.

In contrast, the regular business of a board meeting does not need to be recorded in detail. Many lawyers feel that less detail is better than overly detailed minutes. The minutes may lead to an unwanted blueprint if a nasty plaintiff's lawyer decides to come after you for some reason. In general, you want the minutes to be detailed enough to show that the board was focusing on the right issues, but not detailed enough to allow someone to nitpick the meeting later.

Sample minutes might look like this:

[INSERT NAME OF COMPANY]

MINUTES OF A MEETING OF THE BOARD OF DIRECTORS

[Insert Date of Board Meeting]

A meeting of the Board of Directors (the ***"Board"***) of [Insert name of company], a [Insert state of incorporation] corporation (the ***"Company"***), was held on [Insert date of board meeting] at the offices of the Company.

Directors Present:

[Insert names of directors present]

Also Present Were:

[Insert names of other people present]

Directors Absent:

[Insert names of directors absent]

Counsel Present:

[Insert names of legal counsel present]

NOTE: It's generally good to note next to the above listing if the attendee(s) participated via telephone. Otherwise, it's assumed they participated in person at the above referenced location

Call to Order

[Insert name of CEO or board chair] called the meeting to order at [Insert start time of meeting] and [Insert name of secretary] recorded the minutes. A quorum of directors was present, and the meeting, having been duly convened, was ready to proceed with business.

CEO Report

[Insert name of CEO] reviewed the agenda and welcomed everyone to the meeting. Next, [Insert name of CEO] discussed the current status of the company and its progress. A number of questions were asked and extensive discussion ensued.

Sales & Business Development Update

[Insert name] next provided an update on the overall sales progress and sales pipeline of the Company. He also presented the status of business development discussions.

* [Insert name] joined the meeting.*

Financial Review

[Insert name] provided a comprehensive update on the Company's financial plan and forecast. [Insert name] also reviewed the Company's principal financial operating metrics. Discussion ensued.

Financial Planning

The Board next discussed the timing and creation of the [Insert year] Operating Plan.

Approval of Option Grants

[Insert name] presented to the Board a list of proposed options to be granted to Company employees [and advisors], for approval, whereupon motion duly made, seconded and unanimously adopted, the option grants were approved as presented in Exhibit A.

Approval of Minutes

[Insert name] presented to the Board the minutes of the [insert date of previous board meeting] meeting of the Board for approval, whereupon motion duly made, seconded and unanimously adopted, the minutes were approved as presented.

*Management was excused from the meeting *

Closed Session

The Board next discussed a number of strategic topics. Questions were asked and answered.

Adjournment

There being no further business to come before the meeting, the meeting was adjourned at [Insert time of adjournment].

Respectfully submitted,

_____

[Insert name of secretary], Recording Secretary

NOTE: If attendees join after the meeting start time or leave before the meeting adjournment, it's preferable to note when they join and leave the meeting as indicated above by the asterisked notations.

After reading our sample minutes, you may be thinking, "What on earth are these actually good for?" In litigation situations where a board was accused of not paying proper attention to a company's situation, the simple minutes are often enough to show that the board had appropriately discussed the issue. Make sure you have outside counsel advising you on the level of detail, especially around formal voting matters.

Remember that you need a quorum of the board to take an official vote on anything. Usually, a quorum is simply a majority of the board and a motion requires a majority of the attendees to pass. If you don't have a quorum present, you actually don't have an official board meeting and can't take any official actions.

UNANIMOUS WRITTEN CONSENT

Besides taking official votes at board meetings, the board may also act by unanimous written consent. This is a document that is prepared by your lawyers that looks exactly like what the minutes would look like for a particular vote. The only difference is that that the board isn't together during a meeting, rather approving asynchronously, via signatures to a document.

Keep in mind that you need unanimous consent in order to properly authorize an action this way.

CHAPTER TEN

LEGAL CHALLENGES

As Kurt Vonnegut wrote in *God Bless You, Mr. Rosewater*, big transactions and treasures attract lawyers. Egos and the opportunity for riches, essential ingredients of every good company, often draw out primal attitudes in humans. When conflict arises, lawsuits often follow. When this happens, they are a distraction and a drain on resources, yet an inevitable part of the startup journey.

WHEN THE GOING GETS TOUGH

In most startup companies, many of the board members are also major shareholders. This creates a challenge in some situations, especially with venture capitalist (VC) directors, as the directors are responsible to all shareholders, while at the same time responsible to their investors. If the directors as a whole aren't careful, their behavior, especially in difficult situations, can result in litigation.

Table 10.1 contains a few examples of where conflicts arise and the most appropriate role of the board in resolving them.

If a board is going to be sued by outside shareholders, it's often for one of two things: breach of duty or self-dealing. A judge at Delaware Chancery court pointed out that "90% to 95% [of lawsuits] are a result of a breach of fiduciary duty."[1] In this case, the accusation is that the board was not thinking and acting in the interests of all shareholders. To prove that a director breached his duty, courts like to see specific examples where directors consciously disregarded their duties and acted in bad faith.

Begin by asking if the board had all the necessary information to make an informed decision in a timely manner. If yes, the board has demonstrated *duty of care*. Next, ascertain if any of the board members had a personal or

TABLE 10.1 Examples of Typical Conflicts

	Type of Dispute	Examples	Role of the Board
Founders vs. Founders	Equity ownership	One founder believes another should get less or more equity.	Act in the interest of the company.
	Performance	One founder believes he is single-handedly developing the product.	Act as a peace broker. Resolve in the context of any formal agreements with the founders.
Founders vs. Investors	Control issues	The board ousts the founder CEO, or the board decides to change direction of the business while the founder disagrees.	Ideally, the board would develop a transition plan, identify a replacement CEO, and work with the outgoing CEO on the transition.
	Economic issues	Down rounds and liquidation preferences push founders and common stock holders economic outcomes to zero.	Board demonstrates that they acted in the best interest of all shareholders.
Investor A vs. Investor B	Self-dealing	One group of investors believes that another group enriched themselves at the cost of other shareholders.	The board has to demonstrate they acted in the best interests of all shareholders.
Startup vs. Outsiders	Patents, employment, breach of contract	Infringement of patents, wrongful termination of employees, breach of contracts, and fraud.	The board provides guidance to the CEO and helps him navigate through the various issues.

vested interest in the transaction. If not, the board has demonstrated *duty of loyalty*. However, this won't be true in a VC-backed company, in which case the question can be reframed as "did the board make the decision with reasonable belief that these actions are in the best interests of the company?" If yes, the board has demonstrated *duty of loyalty*.

Self-dealing, simply defined as "sitting on both sides of the table," occurs when a board member enriches himself at the cost of the company. Squeezing more shares out of founders or common shareholders in inappropriate conditions, collecting fees, or giving family members not qualified to help the company consulting agreements are some ways that self-dealing shows up. Self-dealing can be spotted relatively easily, as there is always economics of some sort—either money or shares—involved. Orbotix CEO Paul Berberian says, "The way VCs should make more money is by everyone making lots of money. But often, VCs make more at the cost of other shareholders making less. You have three situations that could pan out—unfair to VC, unfair to entrepreneur and the middle ground—and the middle is where there is a lot of contention."

Following are examples that fall into the gray area of self-dealing and need to be vetted carefully by the board.

> *The controlling shareholders loan money to the company and then foreclose soon after.* Did the directors breach their duty? Likely yes. Depending on how the decision was made and who the interested parties are, a court could view the loan as equity since the controlling shareholders made it. In contrast, if an outside group lent money to the company, the company defaulted, and this group then foreclosed on the company, the board clearly has no control on the transfer and there wasn't self-dealing.

> *A VC suggests another of his portfolio company's performs services for another portfolio company.* If a VC makes the introduction and gets out of the way, that's fine. But if the VC pushes for a stock transaction, prescribes the components of the agreement, and starts to monitor it, it could result in self-dealing. This is especially true if the company providing the services does little work or is an inappropriate vendor for the situation.

MINIMIZING LEGAL CHALLENGES

As a CEO, you can take specific actions to minimize legal challenges and protect against the downside of them when they occur.

For starters, document the process of any major decision. For any decisions made behind close doors, suspicion is bound to occur, especially by those who end up on the short end of the stick. Trust can be broken and credibility can be tainted. By documenting major decisions, you can avoid the "he said, she said" dynamic, especially when conflicts exist.

Make sure you get formal approvals from your board. Then, get the appropriate shareholder approvals. Your outside counsel should follow both the state law in which your company is incorporated as well as the shareholder requirements in your operating agreements.

If the transaction is a major one, get an outside expert, such as an investment bank, to weigh in with a fairness opinion. If you are pricing equity for stock options, use a firm that provides a 409A analysis[2] to provide validation for the price at which you are issuing the options.

PRAGMATIC OR IDEALISTIC?

Often in startups, the only beneficiaries of lawsuits are the lawyers themselves. If you choose to indulge in legal battles and prove that you are right, it may often turn out to be an expensive Pyrrhic victory. However, being practical often translates into faster outcomes with minimum heartburn. Ask the following questions before you engage in a legal battle:

- What is the end game of this legal battle? Is this a fight for principles, or are we being practical? Being righteous while bankrupting the company is idealistic but unsatisfying.
- Is my ego or greed at work here? Am I trying to prove a point to someone? What is more important for the company's benefit?
- What are the anticipated litigation costs, and how will this impact the burn rate and revenues? How much of a time-sink will this be for the operating team?
- What is the worst-case scenario—can you live with the judgment if it is against your company?

Don't ever lose sight of your goal, which should be to build a valuable, long-term company.

PART FOUR

COMMUNICATIONS

CHAPTER ELEVEN

MANAGING ONGOING EXPECTATIONS

Board members have specific expectations around communication from the CEO. A venture capitalist (VC) board member will likely serve on multiple boards and will have seen all kinds of board meetings—good, bad, and ugly. However, CEOs may not have similar broad experience and often learn to manage board expectations in real time. Responsibility for managing expectations around communication often falls to the CEO or the lead director.

WHAT THE BOARD EXPECTS FROM A CEO

It's important to remember that the CEO runs the show. A leader who takes responsibility for his decisions, even if they occasionally turn out to be incorrect, will be highly respected and valued. As CEO, you and your board agree to certain action items, and while the board helps you make decisions, you ultimately have to live with the consequences of the decisions. Weak CEOs hide behind their board, saying things like "the board made me do X" or "the board decided we should do Y," resulting in the CEO's abdicating responsibility for the action taken. This behavior sets up a negative dynamic both with the board and with the management team.

Good boards do not say "We want the company to do thing X." Rather, in each case there is a robust discussion about the topic, and a consensus is reached. In any strong board discussion, participants may disagree and the CEO may not be sure what to do; but, ultimately, a good board reaches a decision and moves on.[1] If, as CEO, you don't agree with the board on a decision, make sure you present your case well. But if you agree to a decision, then it's your decision to own.

The only real operating decision that a board ever makes is to fire the CEO. Sure, the board and individual board members are often involved in many operational decisions, but the ultimate decision is, and should be, the CEO's. If the CEO is not in a position to be the ultimate decision maker, he shouldn't be the CEO. And if board members don't trust the CEO to make the decision, they should take one of two actions available to them: either leave the board or replace the CEO.

If you have a board that is constantly telling you what to do, it should be a sign of concern. Costanoa VC managing partner Greg Sands says, "You as founder or CEO live and breathe this business 80 hours a week. We are screwed if you don't know more than we do." In a situation where a board member is constantly directing you to do something, do not hesitate to sit down one-on-one with your lead director and discuss this challenge. At times, it can simply be a style issue from an overbearing board member. In other situations, it could be a critical situation or concern of the board that you are not hearing properly. Either way, as CEO you have a responsibility to be active in this situation, figure out what is going on, and address it directly.

Whether you are mellow or a screamer, you need to be comfortable with yourself. Everyone has different views on the best way to lead. But I find that a lot of first-time CEOs read books and they get an idea of what it means to be CEO. They behave like they think a CEO should, but they are just acting. When the young CEO reads some management book by Jack Welch and thinks, "I need to be Jack Welch," tries to act like Jack, but ends up nothing like Jack Welch. At the board meeting, such shallowness shows and it's a disaster.

The best ones have a gift—they are natural and are sincere and dedicated, which makes them compelling. Further, the best startup CEOs know what they know and know what they don't know. They aren't embarrassed to ask for help. They don't have an ego attachment to knowing everything—but they have an ego attachment to doing it right. And doing it right means getting help, being self-aware, and knowing when to get help—this can be a huge, huge advantage for a young CEO.

Jason Mendelson, Managing Director, Foundry Group

While all boards are different, there are a few fundamental things a CEO should do around board communications. Following are some thoughts on these from Foundry Group managing director, Seth Levine:

Whether the CEO is the chair of the board or not, they in many respects occupy the key leadership position on the board since their actions for the most part drive the board agenda, the board interaction style, and board participation. And while CEO styles are as varied as the number of CEOs out there, there are a few basic things that boards expect from their CEO no matter how the board is organized.

- *Open and honest communication.* There's no substitute for a CEO's being completely honest with his board. Fundamentally at the root of any board/CEO relationship is trust, which the CEO should foster in his relationship with board members. And while the CEO serves at the pleasure of the board, a good board works for the CEO—meaning that they view their position on the board not as one where the CEO does their bidding but rather where they are there to help the CEO and the business in every way possible. And this can only happen if the CEO is clear, open, and honest in his dealings with the board.
- *Don't manage the board.* In a corollary to being open and honest, it's imperative that a CEO avoids "managing" his board. By "managing" I mean controlling and spinning the information that is passed to the board and being the sole conduit, or bottleneck, to board communication. For starters, it's obvious to board members when they're being managed, and it's impossible to build a trust relationship within that construct. Perhaps more important, a CEO isn't getting the full benefit of the expertise of his board if he's actively managing them.
- *Be prepared.* Be serious about preparing a board package and disseminating information early. Having a good board package that's sent out in advance is part of being properly prepared for a board meeting. So is anticipating questions board members might have, being clear and proactive about what is needed from the board, and encouraging participation at board meetings.
- *No surprises.* It's a cliché of sorts that there should never be a surprise at a board meeting, but in this case the cliché is sage advice. Boards expect not to be surprised by news at a board meeting. Fundamental to an open and honest CEO/board relationship is a CEO's making sure that critical information is clearly laid out to the board prior to a board meeting— always in the board deck and sometimes by phone.

- *Don't have the board meeting before the board meeting.* Good CEOs are in regular communication with their board—between meetings and often right before board meetings. This builds trust, provides important feedback to the CEO, and helps avoid surprises. But good boards expect that the board meeting happens at the board meeting and not in private phone calls with each director. The board meets together to share collective experience and to build on the advice and ideas of each other. Calling each board member before the board meeting to "walk them through the deck" isn't just a waste of time; it robs the board of the ability to function as a group and as a result robs CEOs of the true collective wisdom of the group.
- *Make requests and make them clear.* Good boards and good board members expect and want to be helpful. Good CEOs make this job easier by being clear about what they need help with and making specific requests to board members for their help. And avoid the "please help me sell more" requests, which are both too general and for the most part not what the board is there to do. If you need your board to sell for you, take another look at your sales organization.

Someone once said to me that the CEO has the loneliest job in the world. And in many respects, that's true. However, the board exists to help alleviate that by giving CEOs a sounding board for ideas and a peer group with whom to interact. Critical to a strong relationship between a CEO and his board are these key building blocks that allow boards and CEOs to interact openly, efficiently, and effectively.

Seth Levine, Managing Director, Foundry Group

Good boards care about growing the business, addressing critical issues in an intellectually honest way, with a regular cadence of communication. They also care about your ability to attract customers and team members and execute on your financial plan. But good board members often do not care about the trivial things. VictorOps CEO Todd Vernon recalls when he was CEO for the first time:

I was actually kind of worried—did I spend too much money on my laptop? Are they going to think, "Holy cow—he's just raised this round and is buying crazy stuff!" In retrospect, it's so stupid but I distinctly remember having that feeling. The board has essentially hired you to build a very large, meaningful, fast-growth company—they don't care about something like laptop expenditures.

Rally CEO Tim Miller echoes this sentiment:

> In my first board meeting many years ago, I was concerned that the board might be worried that my wife was in charge of the money and I was in charge of the company, so I spent 30 minutes going line item by line item on financials with rigorous detail. Telephone expense, rent expense,. . . . and the board said, "Hey, we trust you, and we wouldn't have given you $3.5 million if we thought you were going to steal the money." I had no idea what to expect—I tried to put myself in their shoes and offered this level of detail, which they did not care about. Now, after raising $70 million, I don't worry so much anymore.

COMMUNICATE BOTH GOOD NEWS AND BAD NEWS

Greg Gottesman, Madrona Venture Group's managing director, points out that adversity forges strong bonds between the CEO and the board:

> I think many CEOs have a tendency to want to communicate only if there's good news. If there's bad news, you try to fix things. I think the best CEOs are ones who step up the communication when things are difficult, not just when things are going well. And that builds a lot of trust and credibility. It's as simple as seeking a board member's advice one-on-one, outside of the board meeting. It's something as simple as saying, "Hey, I'm just looking for some advice. Here's what's going on." Boards are composed of very smart people; they're big boys and girls, and they can handle the truth. So being truthful and up front builds credibility.

Ryan McIntyre, managing director of the Foundry Group, adds, "If you are selling at all times, or only showing board members the gloss and glitter and none of the warts, you are headed for a disaster. If there's any sort of delay in communication—if there's a difference in speed with which good news gets shared versus bad news—that will ultimately lead to problems."

How often should you communicate? It depends on the stage of the startup, the context of your current situation, and the preferences of your board. Consider these two diametrically opposing examples:

Greg Gottesman points out the challenges when a CEO gets too concerned and calls up board members at each step of the way. "I had one CEO who would call me up for every little decision, would copy me on every e-mail. That's not a good use of the board." Greg reminds us that the board members are not your co-CEO.

Trada CEO Niel Robertson has inverted this situation on its head. "We very specifically agreed to communicate constantly. My board gets daily e-mails from me on every stat on the business. I also expect a meaningful response from my board on these e-mails, and that's a lot of work for VCs, but that's what we have agreed upon. That's what we will do. This creates transparency, and my board is operationally involved to an extent. And the best part—there are absolutely no surprises at the board meetings." In Niel's case, by establishing the communication cadence, he draws the best out of his board.

As Manu Kumar, K9 Ventures' chief firestarter, puts it succinctly, "No new information at board meetings." Resist the urge to walk into a board meeting with awesome upside or downside surprises such as "We signed a strategic partnership with IBM that gives us $3 million," or "Facebook just released a new product that competes with us and cut off our access to their API." When things of this magnitude happen, get the information out to your board right as it happens so they are informed and can respond and help if appropriate.

Orbotix CEO Paul Berberian gives a great example in the context of a key management team member:

> I wanted to promote a strong candidate on my team to the COO role—such a decision requires a lot of preparation to get the board aligned, including timing and compensation. After all, this person could replace the CEO if something happens. I was confident in this person's ability, but the board needed more than just a brief discussion and was surprised when I brought it up for a decision without any previous context. Eventually, the board approved the decision, but not at the board meeting when I first brought it up. If you hear a board member say the words, "I don't agree with you, but I will support you anyway," you should know you have screwed up.

One tactic is to overcommunicate bad news. Renaissance Venture Capital CEO Christopher Rizik recalls this dynamic, "One of my CEOs amplifies any negative news much higher and modulates down the good news—it's a delicate balance and he never overdoes it. I find that the state of the company is never as bad and it is always a bit better—this works for us." A CEO who wishes to remain anonymous gives us another example:

> We were caught in a patent infringement lawsuit. When it started, there was no entry on the balance sheet. Eight months later, as we got clarity of the damages, a $300,000 liability was booked on the balance sheet. Now, all of a sudden, the balance sheet gets lopsided and my board goes ballistic: "Where did this come from?" Even though we briefed the board at every step, this liability suddenly was tangible and was accounted for—it created heartburn. I should have overcommunicated that event in hindsight. Good surprises like winning a $5 million account would be digestible, but this was not that case.

THINGS CEOs CAN DO TO GET IN TROUBLE WITH THEIR BOARD

A board has a set of well-defined legal responsibilities. If a CEO does anything that violates the law, you put your board and the individual board members in jeopardy. Understand the law, pay your taxes, don't lie about anything, do not cook the books, don't steal, treat your employees fairly and don't discriminate, don't sexually harass anyone, and make sure your company is in compliance with all state and federal regulations.

A CEO should not negotiate a round of financing, a sale of the company, or an acquisition of another company by himself. In addition to likely violating the formal investment documents you've agreed to, it's a poor negotiating position, as your investors are also shareholders in your company. Furthermore, it's a bad tactic—many of your investors will have more negotiating experience than you and should be resources for helping you improve any deal you are negotiating. Savvy investors know which investor groups make good partners and which ones to avoid. Finally, the board can veto any decision you may have made if it's not perceived to be in the interests of the company.

While you may have some bad days with your board, it's unlikely that you can fire them. As bizarre as this may sound, we know of examples where a CEO had reached his limit of pain with the board and when the board sat him down to discuss bringing in a replacement, he decided to try to fire the board. "He honestly thought he could terminate the board as he had raised the money and knew the various shareholders. The siren songs in his own head started to play, and he thought he could do it all," says a VC who served on this board. This CEO was last seen updating his LinkedIn profile.

WHAT CEOs SHOULD EXPECT FROM THE BOARD

Depending on the stage of the company, you end up with three kinds of boards: a working board, a reporting board, or a lame duck board. Ideally, for a startup, a working board is best, as it doesn't pontificate or ask mindless questions, but instead dwells on critical challenges that a company faces. It doesn't just suggest time-tested solutions but actually helps implement those solutions.

Tim Miller says, "One of the most valuable things the board can do is shape the business on an ongoing basis. They can help you think through the problems and make better decisions." Over time and as the company evolves to a substantially larger company, a working board should morph into a reporting board, which focuses on governance, liability, and regulatory matters.

While boards hold the CEO responsible, the CEO should also hold the board responsible. When a startup attracts three to five seasoned business and technology experts to the board, the CEO no longer functions in a vacuum or can do things in an arbitrary manner. The board should be involved in all major decisions. At the same time, it's the board members' responsibility to engage. A good board will challenge assumptions, question key issues, and dig deep into the data. If you feel like you've got a set of bobble heads at your board meeting, you've got a problem. Engagement works both ways, as it also motivates the CEO and management team. Andreessen Horowitz partner Scott Weiss says, "Prior to a board meeting, there's this big push to get stuff done. I think it's great hygiene for entrepreneurs."

A working board knows that the CEO is ultimately responsible for running the business. As a result, a good working board "works" for the CEO. While the CEO is ultimately responsible to the board, this dichotomy works well when the board members adopt the attitude of "as long as I support the CEO, I work for her." When this dynamic is blurry, or when individual board members feel like the CEO works for them, the working board dynamic quickly breaks down. JumpCloud CEO Rajat Bhargava explores this in more depth:

The board works for the CEO. What? Wait a second. Isn't it meant to be the other way around? Technically, yes, but largely only during two key situations: when they hire and fire the CEO. Outside of that, every CEO should view their board as working for them, and every board member should have the same view—they are working for their CEO.

While CEOs may not manage their board identically to how they manage their internal teams, a board does need to be managed. Regardless of whether the CEO is the chairman or not, it is the CEO's responsibility to maximize the value of the board. And that means partitioning work to each of them. Board members are extremely valuable—and expensive—resources that should be smartly leveraged.

Now what should a CEO expect from these valuable resources? Here are six key items to keep in mind.

1. *Public and private support.* Until a formal decision to change the CEO is made, a board should be unequivocally supportive of the CEO, both privately and publicly. Supportive doesn't mean that the board and CEO should not have hard conversations or tackle performance issues; it just means that the board should be actively working with the CEO to see her and their business succeed. This issue is trickier with a public board and a high-profile company. Many boards have undermined their CEOs and in turn hurt their businesses through public comments. In general, if board members cannot be 100 percent positive on a CEO, they should not be speaking publicly. More important, they should be working quickly to regain that confidence—whether in the existing CEO or by replacing the CEO. Quite simply, a sitting CEO deserves the board's support without equivocation.

2. *Availability.* Board members are busy, but they must be available to help support their company and CEO. Board members are obviously not full-time employees, but depending on the issues that the company is facing, they should be actively involved in the business on a weekly basis. Whether it is conversations with the team or attending meetings or reviewing documents, if board members aren't actively involved in the business, then they aren't being leveraged properly or are not putting in the necessary effort. Any business—small or large—benefits from its board. Every CEO should expect an agreed-upon amount of her board's time.

3. *Strategic advice.* Perhaps what boards are most known for is their strategic counsel. High-quality board members have seen the movie many times before. They can leverage their experience for the CEO's benefit. Choosing board members who have deep domain experience is not

necessary to generate valuable strategic advice. Good board members are focused on asking the insightful questions that force the CEO and team to delve deeper. It also should be noted that CEOs should expect their board members to look for the nuances in each company. Pattern matching advice from other situations is helpful, but as wise board members and CEOs know, each situation is slightly different and deserves their respect in thinking about it differently.

4. *Contacts and relationships.* Almost all board members are accomplished, successful people and executives in their own right. Every CEO should spend time learning about her board members' network, past successes, and areas of expertise. Board members in turn should be constantly thinking of ways their relationships and network could help the business. Board members often travel in different circles than their CEOs, including living in different parts of the country, coming from different industries, and being a part of a different generation. All of these lead to different sets of contacts and relationships, which can be leveraged for the benefit of the business.

5. *Governance.* Of course, a board is there legally and financially to govern a business. Every CEO should expect strong financial and legal discipline from her board. Building these practices in from the beginning of an organization is critical. Many times, board members and CEOs gloss over these fine details only to miss the opportunity to have a deep discussion about how to run the business and ultimately scale it. CEOs should embrace the governance and use it as a mechanism to develop a strong operating culture.

6. *Balance (and harmony).* A tricky part of each board is the interpersonal dynamic. A high-functioning board has a healthy dynamic of push and pull, of aggressive and conservative, of innovation and stability. In short, a high-functioning board is balanced and in sync. No one board member (or group of board members) is so powerful that the others cannot add value. This is perhaps a CEO's single greatest challenge in building a quality board—to assemble a balanced board. Board members should strive to create that harmony where different opinions and voices are heard for every major topic. Even topics where the board is unanimous deserve contrarian thoughts.

Every CEO should expect a board that delivers on these six items. However, it is also the CEO's job to manage the board to achieve these points. Strong CEOs know that it is their responsibility to manage and drive the board to success.

Rajat Bhargava, CEO, JumpCloud

Boards are continuously assessing a company's performance against expected outcomes. The board should be measuring the actual results versus the plan, both quantitatively and qualitatively. The CEO now has a clear set of measures and a group that can help evaluate the measures. One entrepreneur pointed out how his board members were able to influence change in a positive way: "When the initial strategy wasn't working, they pushed for a meeting on what we should do differently. We could easily keep pushing the same boulder up the same hill. They also forced us to be more disciplined about budget and spending plans." Accountability works wonderfully when you are not reporting to yourself. A good board can be your compass as well as your map—it helps set the direction, the pace, and the overall context.

You'll often hear VC board members talk about "pattern matching." Since a VC has sat on numerous boards, his experience can lead to seeing lots of positive and negative patterns. While the lessons from these experiences are often helpful, a VC who relies only on these patterns often misses what is really going on. Andreessen Horowitz partner Ben Horowitz writes about the downside of pattern matching on his blog:

> Experienced VCs have been on dozens of boards and seen thousands of deals. As a result, they recognize patterns of strategy and behavior that generally work, and patterns that generally fail. This is very valuable information for an entrepreneur who, if lucky, sees only one deal in his career.
>
> Unfortunately, many VCs overreach with their pattern matching. Rather than saying, "Most companies that sell at this stage regret doing so, and here's why," they'll say, "Don't sell now, that's a stupid idea." Other commonly expressed and incomplete patterns include "don't hire very fast," "hire faster," "don't build a sales force," "build a sales force," "don't build downloadable software," and "build an iPhone app." None of this is useful input for your specific company. A pattern-matched instruction without a rationale provides very little help.
>
> *Ben Horowitz, Partner, Andreessen Horowitz. Retrieved March 1, 2012, from*
> *http://bhorowitz.com/2010/04/13/four-things-some-vcs-do-that-i-dont-like*

USING YOUR BOARD'S SOCIAL CAPITAL

VCs often have extensive Rolodexes that can be tapped to help your startup. Often, VCs can introduce you to a sales guru who brings much required momentum to sales, or a ninja master who can code like mad. First Round

Capital partner Josh Kopelman says, "A VC should be able to help recruit candidates both through the VC's network but also help to close the candidates that the companies identify themselves. A good VC should be able to open doors at partners' prospects, investors, and acquirers."

CEOs should be thoughtful about the value of specific introductions. Board members, especially VCs, get a sense of contribution when they make introductions, and some end up doing it indiscriminately. As CEO, you need to decide if the introductions are actually valuable to your company and the specific needs you have at the time. Greg Sands, Costanoa Venture Capital's managing partner, says, "A board member should offer tactical ideas around recruiting, business development, and financing. Other than that, most of what they are doing is sanding the gears."

Board members' social capital is most helpful in three situations: financing, sales, and recruiting. As you gear up for a financing, in addition to helping you firm up your plan, your board is an excellent source of credible introductions to new investors. Paul Berberian says, "They can say to another VC, 'you gotta get in'—they can be a salesman for you and can help close the round for you." The VC, assuming he is not overselling the situation, can be a powerful source of credibility and endorsement for a new potential investor.

It's likely that all of your board members will know potential customers for you. Sometimes they are former colleagues, another existing investment, or a large company they've done work with in the past. These introductions are warm ones; use them to your advantage. Some VCs, especially those who are strong salesmen, will be willing to make sales calls with the CEO or attend a sales training session so that they have better insight into the company's sales dynamics. Yet others attend trade shows to introduce the team to potential partners. Operationalizing this can be random, or systematic, as Upfront Ventures partner Mark Suster explains:

Create a Google spreadsheet listing your top customer prospects, biz dev prospects, and other companies you would like to meet. Have a column for "want to meet now, in three months, in six months, etc." Listing the future "meets" will help them understand your future road map and thinking, but will help avoid getting dropped into an exec meeting for which you're not ready

Have a column for board members and investors to put their names against whom they know. This will help because no investor wants to be the one without his name against anybody. VCs compete among each other to show that they aren't the ones not adding value (a nice double negative, but true!).

Have a space where you say, "Please add other useful intros you feel you could make," and encourage them to add more names.

Make sure to politely remind investors to run intros by you before sending them out. VCs want to help and don't want to be unfocused. But most VCs are "intro machines." Help them to be well behaved. Help them to follow your process. If you're polite and persistent, they will—and they'll appreciate it.

Make sure to send a monthly e-mail to all board members and investors with a link to your spreadsheet saying, "I've made a few updates. I'd be grateful if you would quickly check the spreadsheet to see how you could help." VCs will not check proactively without a reminder. They are busy. They want to help, but they barely get through all their e-mail, let alone log into online spreadsheets.

Finally, make sure you print out the spreadsheet and quickly walk through it toward the end of your board meeting. This is partly to help you get the intros you need while you're all in the room. It's partly to remind board members that you walk through it at each board meeting.

Publicly thank any board member in your board meeting for an intro that led to something spectacular. I hate to sound dumb, but VCs are just like any other people, and human behavior is predictable. They work hard to help you succeed. And the reality is that they'll never say they want recognition, but it's nice to be recognized when you went out of your way and it paid off for somebody. That small recognition will help you get a bit more out of your VCs relative to other boards they sit on. I know any VC reading this will be wincing and thinking it isn't true. It is. VCs are all just grown-up big kids who operate the same way we did when we were young. Recognition is Pavlovian.

Mark Suster, Partner, Upfront Ventures

Finally, your board members can help you recruit talent at all levels of the company. Ask your board members to provide leads for candidates for key positions. Make sure they know what roles you are hiring for. If a VC firm has a recruiting partner or staff member within the firm, use them.

BOARD MEMBER AS PSYCHOLOGIST

"There's not a startup in the world that doesn't go through some scary times. How the board responds during moments of stress says a lot about the boards, much more than the moments of success," says Ryan McIntyre: "It's easy to be a cheerleader for a company that's knocking the ball out of the park. But to be constructive when things take a bad turn is a test of the board."

Some CEOs feel that they should never show any weaknesses. One VC remarked that one of his portfolio CEOs once said, "Hey, you need to know this. My father passed away unexpectedly." He shared this news with his board member several days after this event occurred. In this case, the CEO may have felt like it was his job to show no weakness. This board member quickly offered the CEO the following advice: "No one expects you to be a robot, carrying the weight of the world around with no emotion. Things are much easier to deal with when you get them out in the open."

In another situation, a CEO described that he had to deal with a suicidal employee. "So yesterday, this guy has put a gun in his mouth and threatened to kill himself. Two other employees went to his house to talk with him and essentially rescue him from himself. And then today, he shows up to work. What do I do? I can't cry in my chairman's beer."

Niel Robertson says, "The CEO has a tremendous emotional burden—they deal with a multitude of challenging issues every single day. When you see board members come in and make these sweeping gestures—just do this, or fire that person—they are being thoughtless and lacking empathy."

If you develop a trusted relationship with your board members, you'll start to open up with them. It's not the case that the board will become a substitute for a psychologist, but an individual board member may comfortably settle into the role of emotional confidante for the CEO. Optimally, you'll find a board member you trust who never:

- Says, "I told you so. . . ." If there is a differing point of view, he accepts the decision and lives with the consequences. No credit, no blame, just results!
- Tells you one thing in private and the opposite in the boardroom.
- Tries to be right all the time or show you how smart he is; instead, he focuses on making the company successful, not his ego.
- Surprises you or neglects to inform you of something on his mind.
- Sucks up to the lead, or loudest, investor.
- Plays a game like giving the silent treatment or going dark when you disagree with his views.

In communicating, each party should be aware of the other's positions, communicate proactively, and correct any dysfunctions. If all board members care strongly enough about the business opportunity, the culture of communication will be high on the priority list.

CHAPTER TWELVE

TRYING NEW THINGS

While many board members are used to a particular style and rhythm of board communication, there are no hard-and-fast rules for how it should work. As CEO, you should feel free to experiment with different aspects of your board communication, including formality, transparency, and the tempo of the interactions.

As CEO, you should work with your lead director to try new things. You should constantly be learning from others in an effort to improve your board communication and the overall board effectiveness.

CONTINUOUS INFORMATION

As technology has dramatically changed communication patterns, some entrepreneurs and investors have been suggesting new approaches to board communications. One of our favorite entrepreneurial thinkers, Steve Blank consulting associate professor at Stanford, suggests that CEOs take a *continuous information access* approach. In this approach, the CEO and board members communicate on a continual basis, rather than ad hoc or periodically at board meetings. Following is Steve's explanation of this approach:

Founders/CEO should invest one hour a week providing advisers and investors with "continuous information access" by blogging and discussing their progress online in their startup's search for a business model. They would:

- Blog their customer development progress as a narrative.
- Keep score of the strategy changes with the business model canvas.
- Comment/Dialog with advisers and investors on a near-real-time basis.

What does this change?

- *Structure.* Founders operate in a chaotic regime. So it's helpful to have a structure that helps "search" for a business model. The "boardroom as bits" uses customer development as the process for the search, and the business model canvas as the scorecard to keep track of the progress, while providing a common language for the discussion. This approach offers VCs and angels a semiformal framework for measuring progress and offering their guidance in the "search" for a business model. It turns ad-hoc startups into strategy-driven startups.
- *Asynchronous updates.* Interaction with advisers and board members can now be decoupled from the once-every-six-weeks, "big event" board meeting. Now, as soon as the founders post an update, everyone is notified. Comments, help, suggestions, and conversation can happen 24/7. For startups with formal boards, it makes it easy to implement, track, and follow up board meeting outcomes. Monitoring and guiding a small angel investment no longer requires the calculus to decide whether the investment is worth a board commitment. It potentially encourages investors who would invest only if they had more visibility but where the small number of dollars doesn't justify the time commitment. A board as bits ends the repetition of multiple investor coffees. It's highly time efficient for investor and founder alike.
- *Coaching.* This approach allows real-time monitoring of a startup's progress and zero lag for coaching and course correction. It's not just a way to see how they're doing. It also provides visibility for a deep look at their data over time and facilitates delivery of feedback and advice.
- *Geography.* When the boardroom is bits, angel-funded startups can get experienced advice independent of geography. An angel investor or VC can multiply his reach and/or depth. In the process, it reduces some of the constraints of distance as a barrier to investment.

Steve Blank, Stanford Consulting Associate Professor,
www.xconomy.com/san-francisco/2011/06/03/reinventing-the-board-meeting/

LEARNING BY DOING: SERVING ON OTHER BOARDS

For CEOs, the best way to learn about being a board member is to be an outside director for another company. It doesn't matter how big or small the company is—having the experience of being a board member for someone else's company is immensely valuable. A CEO of a fast-growing startup goes through awesome days, dismal days, and lots of in-between days. No startup follows a linear path of progress, and by being a director of another company you will learn many things that will help you be more effective working with your board. Following are a few examples:

Build a detached and objective view of challenging situations. In the role of an outside director, you will see how you could become emotionally and functionally detached from the pressure and dynamics of what the CEO is going through while still understanding the issues. This perspective will build some new muscles for you and give you a much broader view on how the job of a CEO actually works.

Build empathy for your board. You might have new empathy for a CEO, which could include self-empathy since you are also a CEO. This is a difficult concept for some but is fundamentally about understanding yourself better, especially when you are under emotional distress or intellectually challenged. You'd have empathy for other board members and would either appreciate your own board members more or learn tools and approaches to develop a more effective relationship with them—or even decide you need different ones.

Acquire a deeper understanding of board duties and responsibilities. You'll be on the other side of the financing discussions as a board member, rather than the CEO. You'll understand the concept of fiduciary responsibility more accurately. By seeing board duties from multiple vantage points, it will improve your ability to present information to your board while understanding better how they'll receive it.

Build a peer network. You'll have a peer relationship with another CEO where you have a vested interest, at least emotionally, in her success. You'll get exposed to new management styles. You'll experience different conflicts and different pressures. The intellectual challenge provided by this experience will make you a stronger CEO.

To start with, one outside board relationship is appropriate. Not two, not three—just one. Any more than one is too many. As an active CEO, you just won't have time to be serious and deliberate about it. While you might feel that you have the capacity for more, your company needs your attention first. There are exceptions, especially with serial entrepreneurs who have a unique relationship with an investor where it's a deeper, collaborative relationship across multiple companies, but generally one outside board is plenty.

CHAPTER THIRTEEN

COMMUNICATION CONFLICTS

Whether or not you acknowledge it, a CEO gets a continual education in human behavior. This education often manifests itself through the various conflicts a CEO has to mitigate between board members. Some of this is abstract, as in the collision of emotion and logic. Some of this is exogenous to the CEO, but critical nonetheless such as when a venture capitalist (VC) gets fired from his firm but stays on your board. And some of this is highly contentious, such as a direct conflict between a board member and a member of your management team.

EMOTION VERSUS LOGIC

A CEO will often create elaborate logical labyrinths to minimize risk or justify his actions—but as human beings, emotions play an equal, or even dominant role in our decision making. While many people assert that they are driven by data, we often rely on gut feelings, snap judgments, and instinct. We make choices because we think it will please someone, make someone feel happy, reciprocate for something someone else has done for us, or make ourselves feel good. Jonah Lehrer points out in his book *How We Decide*, "Our best decisions are a finely tuned blend of both feeling and reason—and the precise mix depends on the situation."

Now, there is nothing wrong with healthy emotions. Without emotion, it becomes incredibly difficult to settle on any one opinion, and we can fall into the trap of endlessly poring over variables and weighing the pros and cons in an endless cycle of computations. When emotions dominate, it's important to acknowledge that logic isn't driving our thought process. Thus, if you find yourself in a situation where the decisions of the board don't add up, know that it's not always logic at work.

RECIPROCATION

In a classic book on human psychology, *Influence: Science and Practice*, author Robert Cialdini writes that reciprocity is one of the most widespread and basic norms of human culture. Reciprocity is exchange and manifests itself positively (if you give me a gift for my birthday, I'll likely remember and give you one for yours) or negatively ("horse-trading," where politicians vote on someone else's bills just because the other politician supported their bill). Even professionals like doctors are heavily influenced by the notion of reciprocity; they get "consulting agreements" or "paid vacations" from pharmaceutical companies in exchange for prescribing a particular drug.

Consider a five-member board where two of the VC board members have had a long-standing relationship. VCs often syndicate investments and have made or lost money together. This dynamic can be positive, as the two VCs may work well together, but it can also be negative. If a VC brings another VC into a promising investment, the dynamic of reciprocity can begin. During the negotiation process, the VCs might collude to negotiate a better deal for themselves. This adds to what may already be a history of reciprocity that may be opaque to you. While this may have no bearing at the moment of investment, it could have impact on board level decisions later on.

The best antidote for concerns about negative implications of reciprocation is to address it up front, at the time of investment, and put it bluntly to investors, for example, stating, "I know that you have a long-standing relationship and a history of working together and that this could be a huge advantage to our startup. However, how do we make sure this doesn't lead to collusion between the two of you and ultimately hurt the company?"

GROUPTHINK

In groups, we like to conform rather than act independently. Time and again, studies have shown that our behavior changes, at times dramatically, when we are in groups. This can explain why you have some board members who say one thing in a one-on-one session but change their views when they are in the boardroom. This is classic groupthink at work, where the individual doesn't want to be seen as a renegade.

Author David McRaney points out in his book *You Are Not So Smart* that our desire for conformity is strong and unconscious, like the desire to keep everyone happy around a dinner table. But beware of the other side—the dark place conformity can lead to. Dan Ariely writes in his book *The (Honest) Truth about Dishonesty* that group dynamics can decrease the quality of decisions. We have all seen this happen in large organizations and government entities. It's called bureaucracy, and decisions are made via the lowest common denominator approach. No one gets fired, but nothing ever gets done.

Rock stars in the boardroom can add to the problem of groupthink. Imagine the case of a real-life rock star in the boardroom. The lead singer of a famous rock band strides in, lowers his shades, and says, "We really should move away from iOS and look at Android." There would be a chorus of "ayes" followed by "And now can we get your autograph, picture, and a hug?"

More often than not, we subconsciously gravitate toward people who look like us, who agree with or compliment us, or are physically attractive, writes Robert Cialdini. It's called similarity, compliance, association, and co-operation. Such psychological nuances often make one board member persuasive over others, creating a halo effect. These aspects of human behavior may be especially troubling in the context of a boardroom. While they can't be avoided, you need to recognize these and address them directly. Watch for pandering when a VC excessively influences another board member. Make sure you factor this in when you see a vote being cast. You cannot necessarily avoid this situation, but it will help you to play your cards well when you know the pecking order of influence.

If you see groupthink and weak spines around the table, raise your hand and ask, "Are we conforming to look good to each other? Or do each of us believe this is a good decision?"

YOUR VC FIRM INVESTED IN A COMPETITOR

Communication conflicts aren't limited to abstract behavioral constructs. Consider the situation where you raise money from a VC firm. Six months later, a different partner at that firm makes an investment in your direct competitor. Suddenly, the VC firm has a real internal conflict and you have a concern about their behavior and loyalty to your company.

Some VCs will attempt to explain they have a *Chinese wall*, an infamous term from the banking industry that implies that there is no communication between the partners about the two companies. While nice in theory, it's virtually impossible in practice. While you might be happy with the illusion of the Chinese wall, your naïve bliss will be crushed when you receive an e-mail from your VC partner/board member intended for the CEO of the competing company.

There is no ideal answer for this other than being direct about the concern. If the VC offers to leave your board, seriously consider it. If other board members are concerned about the VC firm's involvement in both companies, ask them to address it directly. Don't be in denial, but at the same time search for a constructive answer.

WHAT HAPPENS IF YOUR BOARD MEMBER ENDS UP ON THE BOARD OF YOUR COMPETITION?

This situation gets worse if the actual VC partner ends up on conflicting boards. There's a famous public company case where Eric Schmidt, the chairman and CEO of Google, was also on the board of Apple. This worked fine for a while until Google decided to come out with Android, which competed directly with the iPhone. Steve Jobs famously lost his temper, banished Eric Schmidt from the Apple board, and went on the warpath against Google and Android.

Board members rarely end up on competitors' boards by design. Business trajectories are dynamic, and companies in tangential markets often end up having competitive overlap. They go after the same resources: customers, capital, and talent. Occasionally, the paths of two companies converge.

When this situation happens, each board member has a responsibility under his duty of care and duty of loyalty to proactively disclose these conflicts to both companies. This director should recuse himself from discussions that could be damaging to either company. The director should be especially careful of disclosing confidential information to the other company, as it exposes him and the other company to liability and legal action.

Ultimately, most directors who find themselves on boards of directly competitive companies will almost always choose only one of the boards to continue on. Often, this happens proactively, but don't be afraid to force the issue if you don't see anything happening to resolve the issue.

WALKING DEAD VC PARTNER

One thing to always keep in mind is how externalities will affect you and your board. One externality that may have the greatest effect is when a VC on your board joins the "walking dead."

A "walking dead" VC partner refers to a partner who still has a business card of his venture firm, but is either on his way out of the firm or has been neutered at his firm to where he has no power to get anything done.

The issue that arises with walking dead VCs is the changed dynamic around reputational constraints. While contracts are important in the startup ecosystem, the number one factor that drives behavior is not legal obligations, but reputational constraints given how small the industry is. If reputation is no longer a concern, consider how human motivation changes.

There are several different scenarios regarding the walking dead, so let us examine a few of them. The first type is the walking dead of the variety where a VC is soon to be exited (involuntarily) out of his venture firm. This is usually due to poor investment performance, but also can be related to bad interpersonal dynamics. VCs who are fired from a firm rarely end up at another VC firm. While there are exceptions, most go on to other professions. It's hard enough to raise money as a VC with a good track record; it's almost impossible to raise money or get a job with a bad one.

When a VC knows the end is near for his tenure at his firm, you potentially see two behaviors arise. First, their reputation as a VC has little value to them, as they will be either retiring or going to work in a different industry. Subsequently, they will care less about what the entrepreneurial community thinks of their actions. In this case, you may see the VC becoming erratic, disinterested, or disruptive. In other words, his true colors come out under stress.

Second, you may encounter a situation where the VC is banking his entire VC career on your company. While you may want to sell the company for $100 million dollars, the VC will unreasonably or irrationally veto this idea in hopes of a billion-dollar exit to save his career.

Sometimes this soon-to-exit VC is doing so voluntarily. Perhaps he is going to another firm or retiring. While reputation may continue to matter, realize he likely won't have the same financial interest in your company's outcome and may start to disengage.

Finally, we've seen situations where the VC isn't fired, but rather stripped of power within his firm. This happens more often than people think and can lead to issues where promises made in the boardroom (e.g., "Don't worry about fundraising, I'll lead the next round!") aren't kept in the end (e.g., "Yeah, sorry that you are out of cash, but my partners aren't supportive").

Some walking dead VCs continue to work hard and are able to be effective board members for your companies. Unfortunately, in our experience, this is the exception, not the norm.

WALKING DEAD VC FIRMS

Walking dead VC firms are similar to the walking dead VC partner. This is the situation where the entire VC firm realizes that it won't be raising another fund and despite the partners carrying around business cards and meeting with entrepreneurs, the firm isn't able to continue in business beyond the current fund.

This situation makes your life even more unpredictable than the individual walking dead VC. If the firm is soon to be out of business, one will normally see something similar to the Agatha Christie thriller *And Then There Were None* whereby partners slowly leave the firm in a bizarre sequence with your VC firm–appointed board member changing several times or, in some extreme cases, losing a board member from that firm entirely. Either way, none of this drama helps you or your board dynamics.

Walking dead firms often are either not supportive financially of their companies or are able to provide only a limited amount of financing. Some partners have little incentive to work hard for your success. The firm may decide to obstruct any liquidity event that you may bring to the table, hoping to swing for the fences to save their fund, despite the best interests of the company. As they wind down their firm, they may try to force you to liquidate the company or at least buy out their investment in your company before you are ready because they are tired and want to wind up their firm and don't want to deal with yours.

It takes a long time for a VC firm to wind down. Often, things will drag on for five or more years. By the end, there are usually only one or two remaining partners stewarding the wind-down. In some cases, the assets might even be sold to another firm with which you've had no previous interactions, resulting in your inheriting a new investor.

When you realize you are dealing with a walking dead VC firm, address it directly and clearly. Make sure you understand whom you will be dealing with, what your expectations for their involvement should be, and what the implications of their firm's ultimate disappearance will imply to your company.

INTERPERSONAL CONFLICT BETWEEN BOARD MEMBERS AND MANAGEMENT

Often, you'll run into a situation where a board member has lost confidence in one of your team members. In the best case, the board member is able to have an open conversation with you about it. If you still support your team member, this board member should offer to work with you to help the management team member improve and regain the board member's confidence.

However, some board members end up in a situation with management team members where there is fundamental mistrust and conflict. This usually stems from a member of your team's feeling regularly undermined or criticized by the director. And, when surfaced, the director either avoids dealing with the conflict or amplifies his negative interactions. Unless addressed quickly, this often becomes a deep-seated mistrust of the director by the member of your team, and a fundamental and regularly expressed lack of confidence in your team member.

As CEO, this situation can be extremely uncomfortable. Like most conflicts, it's best addressed directly. Sometimes it gets resolved. But the longer you avoid dealing with the situation, the more likely it is that the management team member will depart, either voluntarily or involuntarily.

IT ALL COMES DOWN TO TRUST

Ultimately, all communication conflicts come down to trust. When one party fundamentally violates this trust, the only resolution is the departure of that party from the system.

Consider the case of a CEO who feels that one of his board members is refusing to trust him. They talk about it regularly, and the board member continues to say that he trusts the CEO. However, the board member's actions aren't consistent with his words—he regularly second-guesses the CEO in public and expresses doubt that the CEO is telling the truth about major issues. Finally, the CEO has had enough, and at a board meeting when the director once again asserts that the CEO isn't being forthright, the CEO asks directly, "Are you saying I am lying?" The board member hedges, but the CEO persists and states clearly to the board, "If I'm lying, I should be fired." The board member continues to hedge, but when pressed, states, "You are correct, I don't believe you." At this point, one of the other board members, who was in the meeting in question with the CEO, says, "The CEO is telling the truth." The CEO then asks for a closed session of the board and explicitly states that he can no longer remain CEO if the board member who doesn't trust him is on the board. The board, consisting of several outside directors, deliberates without the CEO and decides to ask the board member in question to resign, which he does.

In *Do More Faster: TechStars Lessons to Accelerate Your Startup*, Brad discussed his "Screw Me Once" rule. He allows one fundamental trust violation per relationship. When this happens, he issues the equivalent of a yellow card in soccer, and takes on the responsibility for confronting the issue. When it happens a second time, the relationship is over.

Know your boundaries.

CHAPTER FOURTEEN

CEO TRANSITIONS

As discussed earlier, the board really makes only one operational decision: hiring and firing the CEO. While CEO and board conflict can often get resolved, there are points in the startup journey where the board decides it's time for a new CEO for the company. Sometimes this is a surprise to the CEO; other times it's a graceful transition. Either way, it's one of the most significant and intense things that a board takes on.

SITUATIONS THAT LEAD TO A CEO CHANGE

There are a number of specific situations that lead a board to make a CEO change. Some are cut-and-dry, like fraud or other illegal behavior on the part of the CEO. But most are subjective and often result in long, difficult deliberations on the part of the board before making a final decision.

One of the most common situations is when growth of the company stalls. From the outside, the business may look like it's doing fine. But the metrics tell a different story. Development milestones are missed, sales slow down significantly, and the company starts losing its leadership position in the market.

When growth slows, the best CEOs deal with it directly. They aren't bashful about addressing the slowdown and enlisting the board to help determine what to do. While the pressure for results may increase, the worst thing a CEO can do is be in denial or hide from the reality of the situation. "All trouble starts with founders' insecurities and self-esteem issues—if they don't know how to tackle an issue or are afraid to ask for help—and if a CEO does not have the ability to solve a problem, its going to be transparent very, very quickly. Whether a CEO admits it or not, the board is going to know it," says EDF Ventures co-founder Thomas Porter.

Financing challenges is another common situation that leads the board to question whether a CEO has what it takes to continue leading the company. Remember the three things Union Square Ventures partner Fred Wilson says a CEO is responsible for: (1) setting the overall vision and strategy of the company and communicating it to all stakeholders; (2) recruiting, hiring, and retaining the very best talent for the company; and (3) making sure there is always enough cash in the bank. When raising additional capital stalls, a board will often explore whether the CEO is falling down on any of these three things. While not always the case, difficult financings can create stress and can generate conflict between the board and the CEO.

A steady exodus of key people is another signal to a board to dig deeper to see if the CEO is up for the job. While turnover, including on the leadership team, is a regular part of the growth and development of any company, if senior people regularly leave voluntarily for jobs at other companies, this can be a strong signal that something is wrong at the top.

Finally, conflict arises when the CEO and the VC board members are at cross-purposes about the goal of the company. This can be because the CEO wants to sell and the VC board members want to keep growing the business, or because the VC board members want to sell and the CEO wants to keep going. The example of Zappos, which was a successful exit, shows a positive way that this can be resolved.

We had a tough time convincing our board of directors, who were also our investors, to embrace many of our activities that would help build the Zappos brand and make the world a better place. The directors didn't fully understand or were not convinced of things like brand or culture, dismissing many of these as "Tony's social experiments." Sequoia expected an exit in five years and hadn't signed up for these additional things. I was pretty close to being fired from the board. I was learning that alignment with shareholders and board of directors was just as important.

Tony Hsieh, CEO, Zappos,
Delivering Happiness: A Path to Profits, Passion, and Purpose

SCALE UP WITH GROWTH, OR YOU WILL GET SCALED OUT

In a survey of 212 companies conducted by Harvard Business School professor Noam Wasserman, by the time the ventures were three years old,

50 percent of founders were no longer the CEO; in year 4, only 40 percent were still in the corner office, and fewer than 25 percent led their companies' initial public offerings (IPOs). In a separate study, this theme is validated even though some outcomes are different. Professor Steven Kaplan of the University of Chicago Graduate School of Business, studied 50 venture-backed companies that evolved from business plan to IPO and found that management turnover is substantial. Founders get eliminated quickly along the way: only 49 percent of the VC-backed founders stayed until the IPO.[1] "The entrepreneurs should not be fooled into believing that the VCs care more about them than the company—we just hope this is to be done in a respectful way," asserts Graphicly CEO Micah Baldwin.

As a startup entrepreneur, it's all about your range and how far you can take the startup. Rally Software CEO Tim Miller says, "The single most important question I got from a board member was 'can I take this startup to 200 people? To 1,000 people?' I took it as a challenge. Over the past eight years, I think I have grown tremendously with the help of a good board."

As discussed earlier, a fundamental question entrepreneurs need to ask themselves revolves around the overall theme of this book: economics and control. Do you want to make money or run a company? Or do both? As Noam Wasserman puts it, "If you don't figure out which matters more to you, you could end up being neither rich nor king." In fact, Wasserman's advice is to the point: if you care about control, just bootstrap your business. Relinquishing control comes with the VC territory.

WHY BOARDS FIRE CEOs

There are a variety of reasons that boards fire CEOs. Some are good and rational, while others are bad and capricious. A few common examples follow:

The CEO is a control freak. A CEO was fired because, despite his performance, he was a control freak. "No decisions could be made by anyone—it became quite unnerving as we looked at the challenges in attracting A players. We finally decided to fire the CEO in the long-term interests of everyone," says the VC who served on the company's board.

The CEO is directionally challenged. A startup, receiving rave reviews in scientific and business media, established its market direction in the diagnostics arena. As the new CEO came on board, he saw a compelling opportunity in the defense sector and wanted to shift directions. "He almost hijacked the company. Three months into his role, we didn't feel right, and six months later, we knew for sure this was the wrong guy," says the chair of the board. After burning through millions of dollars, the CEO was fired. The company suffered a down round in its next financing event. It took six years for the company to recover, but it was eventually acquired for over $200 million. The opportunity in diagnostics prevailed even as defense spending dried up.

The CEO does not scale. As a company was growing, the founding CEO was on his third startup but could not scale. He was always sitting in his neat corner office and never took the time to understand the product intricacies. He dropped prices when it was unnecessary, compromising the financial future of the company. This manufacturing process required the ability to manage vendors and inventory as well as maintain productivity. The founding CEO was a creative type but had lost his enthusiasm as well. "How can a CEO who is making something so exciting sound so dull and boring?" a prospective investor asked a board member. The discipline and operational skills required to scale the company were utterly lacking. "Even though we were doing so well, we didn't see this CEO taking the company to IPO," says a VC board member. But it would take over a year to get the board aligned to replace the CEO.

It's time for change. One entrepreneur we interviewed pointed out that he was ousted when the Series B financing was raised. Apparently, the Series B investors believed that replacing a CEO would accelerate the company's growth. The new CEO was brought in and did not perform. This led to another CEO change about 18 months later. The company eventually folded. "We had three CEOs in three years. I felt the board wasn't familiar with the market and we ended up with inaction or conflicts rather than quick decisions. I felt some board members were unfamiliar with the business: they were financial investors who didn't have much startup experience," he says.

A stronger CEO becomes available. A first-time CEO started a life science company and steadily built it over a period of five years, raising multiple venture rounds. However, she was replaced when a highly accomplished candidate (a CEO who had an IPO and two successful prior exits) became available. The founder had no exits as yet. Since the candidate had deep relationships with potential acquirers and had demonstrated ability to sell companies, the board promptly voted to replace the founder and bring the candidate in as CEO.

The chairman's son needs a job. The lead investor and chair of the board fired the CEO and planted his young son as a CEO, helping him to learn the business at other investors' expense.

The CEO cannot enter the building. A VC we interviewed shared that a CEO of one of his portfolio companies could not enter the building due to a pending harassment case initiated by one of the key employees. The board and VCs tried to build on the second layer of management by asking the CFO to step up.

The problem lies on both sides—while entrepreneurs are slow to recognize their own shortcomings and ask for help, VCs are often too quick to jump the gun and seek change of guard. Manu Kumar, K9 Ventures' chief Firestarter, says, "VC behavior reminds me of that song 'If I Had a Hammer.' Unfortunately, most VCs have a hammer and the unfortunate nail is the CEO. A company's problems do not necessarily go away by firing the CEO—at times that may be the worst of all options." When a startup hits a ceiling (or bottom), VCs want to hire a new CEO. A new CEO may not necessarily have the same passion, sense of commitment, or deep domain expertise.

> sigmaalgebra: How does a Board handle a CEO as strong, opinionated, radical, and socially awkward as, say, a young Bill Gates, Steve Jobs, Larry Ellison?
> Fred Wilson: Gently.
>
> *Fred Wilson, Partner, Union Square Ventures,*
> www.avc.com/a_vc/2012/02/mba-mondays-series-the-board-of-directors.html

PLANNING FOR HEALTHY TRANSITIONS

CEO transitions can occur under a few predictable circumstances, and it's beneficial to both sides—the board and the CEO—to formulate a simple outline that can allow for this transition to be conducted with minimum grief and drama. Following are some of the things that a board should communicate to a CEO in this context:

Performance. Establish annual metrics of CEO performance in conjunction with the board. A CEO should be able to control as well as impact these metrics and have adequate resources to execute the plan. The CEO knows the warning signs of performance: the metrics start to falter.

Chemistry and cohesion. While performance matters, as companies grow, the ability to build a cohesive team of high performers is equally important. The best CEOs attract fantastic people. However, CEOs who are unable to delegate attract mediocre people.

Decision-making process. The board should offer warning signs to alert the CEO of lack of performance or team issues. While startups do not have the cash cushion or the luxury of extended periods of performance remediation, the relationship with the board will determine how these are communicated to the CEO.

When the transition is a healthy one, Thomas Porter says, "Founders should absolutely have a say in picking the next CEO, if and when they are being replaced. But this should be earned by building a trusting relationship with the board. Knowing who you are, your values, and the trajectory you seek for the company will help you find the right CEO."

Once the decision has been made to part ways, the CEO and board should work together to communicate this appropriately to the team members. Such situations can be highly emotional, and some CEOs, especially when they are founders, can have a negative reaction. If this happens, the healthy transition often goes awry, and the CEO is subsequently escorted out of the building. Obviously, it's in both the board's and the CEO's interest to work together to not let the situation deteriorate.

In some situations, a founder/CEO may easily shift into a new role. A classic example is the technical founder/CEO who shifts to chief technical officer (CTO) when a new CEO joins the team. Another case is the CEO who becomes executive chairman, staying actively engaged with the business in a non-decision-making role. If the transition is smooth and harmonious, such role changes can lead to stronger outcomes for the company.

BOARD TRANSITIONS

As the company grows, its revenues or business model may collide or impinge on the path of another board member's business. This can cause challenges for both parties. Board members who recuse them-selves with full disclosure are a rarity, but as the businesses begin to overlap, it's often necessary to effect change. In other situations, board members need to be eliminated if they fail to perform basic duties, are unable or unwilling to help with meaningful inputs, or create dishar-mony and angst.

The case of tech entrepreneur Mark McCue's leaving the Twitter board was speculated to be a function of the potential collision course between the two companies. Kara Swisher wrote, "The reason, sources said, is McCue's growing feeling that the companies are on a product collision course, with a possible troubled or perhaps more attractive result. In other words, Flipboard will either face increasing rivalry from Twitter or will end up as a possible acquisition target for it."[2]

An older but more dramatic example is when Arthur Rock, noted angel investor, was a board member at Apple and Intel. "Apple took a two-page ad in every newspaper you could think of, announcing that they were ready to ship the PowerPC, which I did not know they were going to manufacture— but that's not important—but that they were going to kill Intel. Literally— that's what it said. At that point, I resigned."[3]

GETTING RID OF THE ENTIRE BOARD

As successful as Apple may be, its boardroom dynamics are complicated. When Apple's board brought back Steve Jobs after the company almost went bankrupt, Steve immediately started to work his ways. He did not respect his board and bluntly said, "This company is in shambles and I don't have time to wet-nurse the board. So I need all of you to resign. Or else I am going to resign and not come back on Monday."[4] After the board resigned, Jobs brought in Larry Ellison, founder of Oracle, who hated meetings and came to only a third of the board meetings. Jobs had a life-size cardboard cutout picture of Larry put in. Over the years, Jobs brought strong people on Apple's board, like Al Gore, Eric Schmidt of Google, and Bill Campbell of Intuit.

Biographer Walter Isaacson writes, "He always made sure they were loyal to a fault. Despite their stature, they seemed at times awed or intimidated by Jobs, and were eager to keep him happy." Jobs even invited the former chairman of the SEC, Arthur Levitt, but then found that Arthur was a huge proponent of strong and independent boards. Jobs promptly uninvited him, saying that Levitt's views did not apply to Apple's culture.

Getting rid of your entire board may sound like a good idea especially during a dark moment when you are particularly frustrated with your board, but it's highly unlikely you will be able to pull this off in a VC-backed startup. It's a move that can backfire, and it's best for you to consider leaving the company if you have fundamental and unresolvable differences with your entire board.

PART FIVE

TRANSACTIONS

CHAPTER FIFTEEN

FINANCINGS

The dynamics around a financing can vary dramatically, but your board always plays a key role in the process. While board members, especially VCs, can play an active role in raising the money, finding new investors, and negotiating terms, they also have an extremely important governance role.

Every financing has formality around it. Legal documents, including a stock purchase agreement, must be negotiated and signed. The board must approve formal resolutions associated with the financing. And numerous documents need to be signed by each board member.

As with any transaction, it's critical to have an experienced lawyer involved. Your brother-in-law who specializes in divorce law isn't the right choice. Make sure you have experience on your team.

We aren't going to go into financings in depth—for that, read *Venture Deals: Be Smarter than Your Lawyer and Venture Capitalist*. However, we will explore several different situations and the unique responsibilities of the board in each one.

NEW INVESTOR-LED ROUND

The simplest financing transaction is one where there is a new investor leading the round. In this case, the board's duties are straightforward, since the conflicts are limited because an outsider, who has no prior interests in the company, is driving the terms. There will be a long list of resolutions associated with the financing, but these are standard and rarely controversial.

As with any transaction, there is value to formality. A board meeting should be held, attendance taken, motions proposed, and votes taken. These resolutions should then be memorialized in the minutes.

INSIDE-LED ROUND

When an existing investor leads a round, especially when that investor also has a board seat, there is potential for conflict. The key concern is whether the pricing is "fair to all shareholders" and the directors have fulfilled their duty of care to the company.

In an inside-led round, it is important that all board members, especially the outside directors, participate in the deliberations. The investor/board member who is leading the round should explicitly acknowledge his conflict and the non-conflicted board members should be able to freely express their opinions.

Ultimately, the voting dynamics will be dependent on the rights in the certificate of incorporation, as defined by whichever voting rights agreement was executed in the earlier financing transaction. If the round is done at a price equal to or greater than previous rounds, the main focus of the discussion should be on whether the financing is fair and the existing, non-conflicted shareholders support it. While formal approval of all shareholders is unlikely to be required, if there is any concern, a rights offering, which we will discuss in a moment, should be done.

THE DOWN ROUND AND A RIGHTS OFFERING

A *down round* occurs if the price of the new round is lower than the previous round. If a new investor leads the down round, the board doesn't have any special responsibilities beyond those in a typical financing. However, if an existing investor leads a down round, the board needs to be extra sensitive to conflicts.

The best way to address the situation where an existing investor leads a down round is to do a *rights offering* to all shareholders. A rights offering is a legal process that gives every investor a chance to exercise his pro-rata rights—even if he doesn't have formal pro-rata rights.

The best way to execute a rights offering is to do a first close of the financing with the existing major investors and then do a rights offering to all shareholders. While this involves extra paperwork and effort, it eliminates the risk that a minority shareholder might complain at a later date that the financing wasn't in the best interest of the company. This situation is one that you really want an outside board member to bless. Many companies find themselves in this situation without an outside board member, and these transactions have been known to lead to litigation later.

HOW INVOLVED SHOULD VCs BE IN FINANCINGS?

Some VCs claim to have special, magic skills that help any company raise future rounds of financing. While it is certainly true that some VCs are much better at raising money than others, ultimately the financing is the responsibility of the CEO.

A common mistake of first-time CEOs is to expect that once they get a VC on board, they will have an easier time of raising money in the future. This is rarely true—an experienced CEO knows that every financing process is unique, and many are challenging due to circumstances exogenous to the company, such as the macroeconomy, the sudden presence of a new competitor, or the activity levels of target VCs.

A great VC can effectively set expectations with a CEO and the board as to how they can help. Following are some thoughts on this from TechStars' managing director, Mark Solon:

By default, almost every startup that raises money from a VC firm has chosen a path of super high growth. VCs don't invest in startups for CEOs to sit on that capital; they expect the CEO to use it as rocket fuel for growth—products must be developed and markets must be created and penetrated. However, once that path is chosen, rarely is one round of financing enough for the company to reach "escape velocity." Accordingly, subsequent rounds of financing are often needed to sustain the type of growth and scale needed for such a high-growth flight path.

More often than not, the second round of financing presents a scenario that causes some questions for startup CEOs, including "how involved should my existing VC be involved in helping to raise my next round of capital?" Fact is, few

VC firms will finance a company from seed or Series A all the way to an exit by themselves as most don't have enough capital allocated to do that and having another institutional partner at the table brings additional resources to help the company grow. As a result, the first VC to invest in a company will typically like the CEO to raise capital from a new VC firm in order to reduce risk and add resources, even if they're going to contribute additional capital to the round themselves.

It's at this stage where I've seen CEOs become frustrated with their existing VCs. Many have expectations that their VC will magically open doors to additional capital and the process will be smooth and easy. Unfortunately, it rarely happens in this fashion. Does having an existing VC as an investor make it easier to raise subsequent capital? Yes, sometimes. However new firms will do just as much due diligence as the first VC—perhaps even more as the company is no longer raising capital on a vision but now on performance as well.

Many startup CEOs expect their VCs to introduce them to a bunch of other firms that they have close relationships with. What they might not contemplate is that their VC has a large portfolio of companies and they can't create fatigue their co-investors by introducing every single portfolio company to their syndicate partners.

A great solution is for the CEO to create a spreadsheet (Google docs works great for this collaborative exercise) of 20 to 30 firms to reach out to. Some of those will be firms that the VC has connections to and believes will be a good fit, and others will be relationships that the CEO has created or discovered through networking. The VC should then scan that list and take ownership of making a warm introduction to the appropriate firms. They should then work together through the fundraising process and keep the spreadsheet updated, but make no mistake about the fact that raising additional capital is the CEO's job.

Keeping the company capitalized is the most important job the CEO has. As a CEO I worked with long ago once told me, "my most important job is to make sure the company is around tomorrow, a lot of days in a row." Should VCs be involved in subsequent financings? Absolutely. The VC can and should continue to be helpful throughout the process, talking to the interested firms and getting back-channel insight as to how things are progressing. However, a VC has to be careful not to get in "sales mode" when doing this, as it can set off alarms to other VCs that there's something wrong with the company. CEO's should use their VC as a resource, and the VC should absolutely be enthusiastic about helping. Ultimately, however, raising additional capital is the CEO's responsibility.

Mark Solon, Managing Director, TechStars

CHAPTER SIXTEEN

SELLING A COMPANY

O ne of the most frequently asked questions is "When is the best time for a company to sell?" It's a question that is asked every time a company is acquired, and it usually creates a lot of noise by people whose opinions are usually misinformed and, even more so, irrelevant. Jason Mendelson, Foundry Group managing director, says simply that the answer is "when the founders want to sell—period."

Jason calls this the *VC bargain*. He continues, "Unfortunately, many investors do not feel this way. Clearly, a venture capitalist (VC) can be very helpful in advising the founders about past experiences, the current state of the merger and acquisition (M&A) market, and their thoughts around valuations, but when the founders want to sell, it's time to sell the company. Who are we to tell the founders that they aren't allowed to fulfill their dreams and create an event that will change their lives?"

But this isn't solely a one-way bargain. If you take VC money, you have a bargain as well. You have a responsibility to actually work toward a liquidity event. Few companies can expect to go public. Therefore, the acquisition market is the primary way for investors to create proceeds to return to their LPs. Understanding and respecting this is part of the VC bargain.

CONFIDENTIALITY

At the beginning of any M&A transaction, it's likely that the two parties (buyer and seller) will enter into a *confidentiality agreement*. Board members are included in this and have to be particularly careful to respect these confidentiality agreements.

A signed term sheet will often include a *no-shop agreement*. This is an agreement by the seller not to engage in any conversation about selling the company with any other party during a specific period of time, usually 30 to 60 days. Inevitably, when rumors or leaks occur, outside parties such as the press, investment bankers, or other potential buyers reach out to board members. Given the presence of the confidentiality agreement, especially with a no-shop in place, board members should be particularly sensitive to these situations.

Whenever a confidentiality agreement or no-shop agreement is signed, the board should have a deliberate conversation about the presence of the agreement and how each board member should react if contacted by someone regarding the transaction while it is in process.

Finally, board members should be extremely careful in situations where the buyer or seller is a public company, as any nonpublic information disclosure could lead to insider trading, which is a criminal offense.

There are many situations that occur that may trip your confidentiality or no-shop agreement. The most likely one is when an unsolicited offer is presented after your company has already signed a term sheet to be acquired. It's critical that your first call is to your lawyer in this situation.

FIDUCIARY RESPONSIBILITY

As we've stated previously, the board has a fiduciary responsibility to all shareholders. While easy to say, it's often hard for board members who are also VCs to separate their two roles, especially in an acquisition scenario that provides different consideration for different classes of investors.

First and foremost, the board member has a fiduciary duty to the company. We discussed this extensively earlier in this book. At the same time, a VC has a fiduciary duty to his limited partners. In many cases, these fiduciary duties are aligned, but in some cases they are in conflict with each other.

The VC board member should be able to respect his fiduciary duty to the company. If he can't for some reason, he should resign from the board. This has to be done thoughtfully so as to not be disruptive to the transaction. We've been involved in graceful situations, where a VC stepped off the board during the transaction so they could vote as a shareholder. We've experienced others where a VC board member shouted, "I'm done with this—I resign from the board," slammed down the phone, and refused to talk to any of the board members directly from that point forward.

It's easy for emotions to take over in these situations. As a CEO, if you see any of your board members tangled up in their own conflicts, try to enlist your lead director, your lawyer, or an outside director experienced with deals to help you navigate the situation. Always try to de-escalate the conflict, as you'll usually need support of the VC investors to get the deal closed.

YOUR LAWYER'S ROLE

Your lawyer plays an extremely important role in selling the company. In addition to handling the paperwork, a great lawyer is deeply involved in the transaction, helping negotiate the specific terms with the buyer. He's also a calm communicator, helping to resolve internal conflicts as they arise, explain complicated situations clearly, and drive to resolution on ambiguous or contentious situations.

We've worked with many great transactional lawyers over the years. One of the best is Steve Tonsfeldt, a partner at O'Melveny & Myers LLP. Following are Steve's thoughts on the role of a lawyer in the sales process:

A sale of the startup company usually represents the culmination of many years of hard work for the company's employees, management, and board. Many times the exit process is a very positive experience for the startup company participants; sometimes, however, it represents the disappointing end to a difficult life for the company. In both cases the outside lawyer will be a key player. Given the consuming nature of the M&A process, it is likely that the lawyer will be in daily, if not hourly, contact with the group tasked at the company and around the board table with driving the deal to conclusion. How the lawyer functions in this role will have a large impact on the perceived success or failure of the project.

In a startup sale, the outside lawyer is generally charged with coordinating, and at times leading, the due diligence process, the negotiation and preparation of the various transaction documents, and communications with the buyer, the company, and the board. The company's board and management will also look to the outside lawyer to help ensure that the chosen deal strategy and process is legally supportable and defensible if challenged. There is usually a great deal of time and effort that goes into this work. But as I was told early in my career, "flawless execution in a timely manner" should be viewed as a given, as only the starting point in the deal setting. In the end, the "practical advice" and "experience" components of the engagement are the areas that elevate the lawyer from being viewed as simply competent to being an integral member of the deal team.

In that vein, a few aspects of this parallel role are discussed below:

Conflicts are everywhere. Robert Kindler of Morgan Stanley was famously quoted a few years back as saying "We're all conflicted—get used to it" when talking about the investment banking world. The same could be said for deal making in the world of startup companies. There are potential conflicts everywhere. The interests of the preferred holders with their senior position in the waterfall may not necessarily align with the interests of the common holders. Members of management with a carve-out plan in place or change of control benefits may have a different view of a proposed transaction than the rank-and-file employees without similar protections. Outside investors and former employees may have a different view of the appropriateness of large retention packages being offered by the buyer to continuing employees. Outside investors and former employees may have a similar negative view regarding employee requests for equity acceleration packages. One of the most important jobs of the outside lawyer in this context is to identify these conflict situations and then work to mitigate and manage their impact on the deal, through procedural steps or otherwise, to the extent possible. If there is going to be a claim made by a shareholder or employee in connection with a proposed sale of a startup company, it will almost inevitably involve some form of a claim that the "bad actors" were conflicted in their decision making and somehow put their interests ahead of the interests of the broader constituencies they were to represent. In many situations, the conflicts are unavoidable. In those cases, the board and management can help their position by simply acknowledging that the conflicts exist, that others may have a different view regarding their motivations in the decision-making process, and that their decisions will potentially be subjected to extra scrutiny if challenged. The outside lawyer can play a key role in this process.

Balancing the flow of information. Information flow is one of the basic keys to the perceived success of a sale process. But there always needs to be a balance between too much and not enough communication, and different constituencies will have differing needs to be in the middle of the various communication streams. The outside lawyer will usually be in a position to initiate and direct the flow of information on the deal and therefore will need to apply his or her best judgment to ensure that the right decision makers are in the loop at the right times. It is a given that people do not like to be surprised in the deal process, especially by their own deal team. Also, a board that has been periodically informed of the deal's status along the way or how the parties have reached a particular negotiated term on a tricky or complex matter is generally more likely to support the outcome and be in a position to defend the decision if later challenged. This leads to the conclusion that, like most things in life, if one is to err in this area, it is almost always better for the lawyer to err on the side of overcommunicating.

Board members have differing levels of experience in the deal process. As a related point to the "information" issue mentioned above, it is a virtual certainty that not all of the members of the board of directors will have the same level of experience in dealing with the M&A process. Some will have been through many similar transactions in the past and accordingly be very familiar with the terminology, likely issues, and the process in general. For others, this may be their first time through a transaction like this. In those situations, it will be important for the lawyer to communicate things in a way that all of the board members will understand, but at the same time not oversimplify the discussion to the point where the nuance of the issue is lost. Written summaries can be helpful in this context. Sometimes less experienced board members gain a better understanding of subtle points if they can read them and refer back to the summaries at later times.

Keep the process moving. As a general matter, deals have predictable, natural rhythms. Most deals will be extended unnecessarily on both sides unless there is a clearly articulated goal for signing or announcement. However, many of the proposed timelines that are passed around early in the process to the transaction working group border on the irrational. It is important for the lawyer to understand that these aggressiveness timelines may be used for motivational purposes and be aspirational in nature and that it usually is not necessary or even helpful to point out the many places where there is likely to be some slippage in the schedule. All that being said, the lawyer will have a key role in ensuring that the deal is completed in the allotted time periods. To do that, the attorney will need to have a form of PERT chart in his or her head that focuses on the various critical-path, noncompressible steps in the process. If things are getting off schedule, it is important that the board and management understand what is happening and whether there are modifications that can be made to bring things back on the desired schedule. Again, surprises are never a good thing in the M&A process.

The lawyer's demeanor and communication style matter. In most deals, the lawyer is the frontline communicator and negotiator with the buyer and its representatives through much of the process. When the lawyer reports back to management and the board with a summary of these discussions, the manner in which he or she presents the information will have a large effect on how it is heard and perceived. If every time a proposed term is rejected by the buyer the startup's lawyer describes it as an affront to the senses, it is likely that the company's management and board will interpret it as the buyer's being unreasonable. Not every point fits this description. It does a disservice to everyone if this distinction cannot be made. The lawyer needs to be viewed as the company's fearless advocate, but at the same time be viewed as someone who can give management and the board impartial objective advice when requested.

Steve Tonsfeldt, Partner, O'Melveny & Myers LLP

ACQUIHIRE

In recent years, the concept of an *acquihire* has become popular. In this situation, a buyer acquires a company primarily for its employees. As a result, the motivation of the buyer is simply to "hire" the existing founders and employees, rather than value the overall company. Acquihires are popular in downside cases as a way to sell a company "for something" in order to get a graceful exit.

While the term is a trendy one, these transactions are no different than any other sale of a company. The board has the same responsibilities that it has in any M&A situation. While a buyer will likely focus on getting as much of the consideration as possible allocated to employees for retention purposes, the board still has to be deliberate about doing the best thing for all shareholders.

CARVE-OUTS AND 280G

While some acquisitions result in all shareholders making a lot of money, others are less successful. In some cases, companies are sold for less than their liquidation preferences, resulting in all of the consideration in the transaction going to preferred investors and none going to common shareholders and option holders.

In these downside cases, existing management and employees often get nothing unless a specific amount of the consideration is "carved out" by the board. This carve-out has to be agreed to by the preferred shareholders, since it is coming out of their consideration. There is no standard carve-out amount, although you will often see something in the range between 5 percent and 20 percent of the total consideration. Furthermore, the carve-out is almost always allocated only to management and employees currently employed by the company, and is often structured in a way to retain them over the next year or two.

A carve-out is considered a *parachute payment* and is covered in Section 280G of the Internal Revenue Code. As a result, there is a formal process as part of any carve-out to do a "280G election" in order to get an exemption from the parachute tax payments. In this situation, 75 percent of the shareholders not impacted by the carve-out must approve the carve-out to get the exemption from 280G. We highly suggest that you start this process earlier than later as we've seen many deals delayed because of the need to get 280G approvals.

SHAREHOLDER REPRESENTATIVE

In *Venture Deals: Be Smarter than Your Lawyer and Venture Capitalist*, the role of a shareholder representative is discussed in detail. At some point during the acquisition process, the board must consider who will be the ongoing shareholder representative. Following is an explanation of the role of the shareholder rep:

Acquisitions are not actually finished when the deal closes and the money trades hands. There are terms such as managing the escrow, dealing with earn-outs, working capital adjustments, and even litigation concerning reps and warranties that will last long into the future. In every acquisition, there is someone—referred to as the shareholder representative—who is appointed to be the representative of all the former shareholders in the seller to deal with these issues.

This lucky person, who is generally not paid anything for his services, gets to deal with all the issues that arise between the buyer and the seller after the transaction. These issues can be based around buyer's remorse or be legitimate issues, but are often time consuming, are expensive to deal with, and impact the ultimate financial outcome of the deal.

Traditionally, either an executive from the seller or one of the VC board members takes on this role. If nothing ever comes up, it's a complete non-event for this person. However, when something goes awry where the buyer makes a claim on the escrow or threatens to sue the former shareholders of the company, this job often becomes a giant time-wasting nightmare. The shareholder rep, who typically has a full-time job, limited money from the deal (often tied up in the escrow) to hire professionals to help him, and usually isn't a subject matter expert in anything that is at issue, ends up being responsible for dealing with it. If it's an executive of the seller, he might still be working for the buyer. In any case, this person is now making decisions that impact all of the shareholders and subsequently ends up spending time and energy communicating with them. Finally, some buyers, in an effort to exert even more pressure on the system, sue the shareholder rep directly.

We've each been shareholder reps many times. Several years ago, we decided never to be shareholder reps again, as we see no upside in taking on this responsibility.

If you somehow end up being the shareholder rep, make sure you negotiate a pool of money into the merger agreement that you can dip into to hire professionals to support you should something arise that you have to deal with. We often see a separate escrow that is used exclusively to pay for the expenses of the shareholder representative. If nothing else, this works to be a good shield to a bad-acting buyer since it will see that you have money to hire lawyers to yell at its lawyers.

Never ask someone who will be working for the buyer post transaction to be the shareholder rep. If you do this, you are asking this person to get into a winner-takes-all fight against his current employer, and that is not a happy position for anyone to be in. The only time this ever works is if the shareholder rep has a role that is critical to the buyer where the threat of the rep quitting will help influence the outcome in a way positive to the seller. Regardless, this is a stressful and uncomfortable position to be in.

You should also be wary of letting a VC take on this role. Escrow and litigation dynamics are time sensitive, and we've had experiences where other VCs involved as the shareholder rep paid little or no attention to their responsibilities since they didn't fully understand or appreciate the legal dynamics surrounding their role. We've had some bizarre experiences, including a shareholder rep who was a VC (a co-investor in a deal with us) who blew an escrow situation by ignoring the notice he received from the buyer that a claim had been breached. The notice period was 30 days, and 31 days after receiving the notice, the VC received another letter saying the escrow had been deducted by the amount of the claim. Fortunately, we had a good relationship with the lawyer on the side of the buyer and were able to get an exception made, but the buyer had no obligation to do this other than as a result of goodwill that existed between the parties.

As a result of our experience with this over the years, Jason co-founded a company called Shareholder Representative Services (SRS; www.shareholder-rep.com), an organization that acts as a shareholder rep. The cost, relative to the overall value of the deal, of using a firm like SRS is modest, and you get professionals who spend 100 percent of their time playing the role of shareholder rep. When there is litigation, they get sued and deal with all of the details. Given the wide range of deals they've worked on as shareholder reps, they tend to have wide-ranging and extensive experience with both buyers and their lawyers.

Brad Feld and Jason Mendelson,
Venture Deals: Be Smarter than Your Lawyer and Venture Capitalist

CHAPTER SEVENTEEN

GOING PUBLIC

I f your company is a huge success and the market allows it, you may have the opportunity to take your company public in an initial public offering (IPO). As you march toward an IPO, the board responsibilities take on another level of formality. The level of work increases, the presence of lawyers playing an active role is noticeable, and committee work shifts from informal to formal.

While this is an exciting time for a company, the transition from a private company to a public company is a serious one. The responsibility of public-company directors is well beyond the scope of this book, but as you gear up to go public, there are some specific things that directors should do and pay attention to. Following are some thoughts from Rally Software CEO Tim Miller, who recently took his company public:

As CEO, you should be prepared to share your challenges: be clear about your needs and be vulnerable about the issues you're struggling with. This is different from reporting what you think your board wants to hear. Ask for feedback and be open to what you get back.

You need to put issues into context for your board. For example, with a particular issue you might be thinking, "I don't have a clue and I need your help"; or "I think I know but need your dialogue"; or "I want to inform you about this decision I've made." Tell your board ahead of time which context it is so they know how to give you feedback.

Boards are great at helping you solve a problem that you're seeing for the first time because odds are that they've seen it many times before. Here's an example. Before I started working with Ryan Martens (Rally Software CTO/founder), I wanted to do another company and I had two goals: I wanted to raise venture capital so we could grow a bigger company, and I wanted a great lead director. Luckily, I was able to do both.

Having a great lead director, with the hundreds or thousands of decisions you make as an early CEO, means you don't have to ask five people and get five different opinions. You just ask somebody who can give you the synthesis of the five different opinions, and then you can tweak it a little bit and make it your own. You save so much time and energy and you make pretty good decisions, guaranteed.

There's a time where you start building a board to become a successful public-company board. For me, that was a phase change in how I thought about the board. Prior to going public, board membership was a coveted role whose price of admission was financing. In our case, we did enough financing that we had a full board without the need for additional independents as we grew.

I think it's important to get a team that you think you can work with, and who can add a lot of value at a strategic level. You want to have a "matrix of capabilities" outlining the characteristics you want your board members to bring: knowledge of compliance issues, key competencies, and personal attributes.

For example, you want a CEO type with deep operational experience. You'll probably want an industry expert and maybe a marketing or sales expert. Sometimes you have a technology expert.

Once you're public you'll need a lead independent or a non-CEO chairman. We chose to have a lead director, but in many ways they are like a chairman. "Independent" in this context essentially means not a significant investor or shareholder. CEOs need an outside board leader who can coach them and in whom they can confide. It's important to have a go-to person on your board with whom you can be completely trusting and transparent, to discuss delicate issues such as executive team, employee, or even personal issues that can affect the company.

I recruited Tom Bogan as a board member for a long time, and he's now our lead independent director. Tom was the first person I pitched in our series B funding round in 2005, and we finally got him four years later by simply continuing to pitch him and talk to him from time to time to get his feedback on the product and the business. Tom was president and COO of a similar company called Rational Software, which was acquired by IBM, and he chairs the board of Citrix. So he had a lot of domain knowledge, and he was an operating executive and leader, and he was also a VC. I didn't get him the first time and I didn't get him the second time, but I finally got him the third time—he finally gave up and said, "I gotta do this."

The way I've been trained in my job as a CEO is that you always hire the best candidate. What I've been learning from a corporate governance standpoint is that you don't hire people to a board simply because it "looks good." You might open a diversity rec with the belief that a diversity candidate might provide a unique quality, just like you want a CEO type and an audit committee chair and an industry expert.

I think you can quantify the value of diversity on a board. Diversity brings a different perspective—culturally; experience-wise; how people process, think, communicate, and collaborate; how people best represent their customers and employees and communities, all the stakeholders—and the better representation you have around your board team, the better you'll be able to build your company.

You really want to build a collaborative, high-trust, transparent board before you go public. You want to be able to share everything. You want to overcommunicate with your board. You want the board to get to know you, the CEO, and the management team, as deeply as possible. You need to get them understanding and engaged with where you're going. Becoming a public company means you'll tend toward more reporting out rather than asking for help, and the relationship between board members and the CEO will become more formalized.

Once you're public, you have a new constraint, which is what you need to disclose to the Securities and Exchange Commission (SEC) and the public. So you go from communicating a lot and letting the board filter, to communicating what's most important to communicate given the extra amount of information that needs to be communicated. There's a duty to inform the board, and this can easily fill up an agenda. Because public boards have more process and more formality around them, this can squeeze out the "what keeps you up at night" conversations so you need to have open dialogue and one-on-ones to help shape your thinking outside of and in between board meetings. Board business has to get done, so you lose some flexibility, and you may lose some of the unfiltered transparency that comes from coming in and just "talking."

I believe that a highly collaborative board is more effective at solving the problems and challenges and exploiting the opportunities that a company may have. The two fundamental elements of a highly collaborative board are trust and respect. You have to build trust and work on it over time. It's a cliché, but it takes a long time to build trust and a short time to lose it. One of the ways you build trust is to be respectful: valuing people's input, not shutting them down, treating people as if they're important to you. Being transparent causes trust to happen faster.

A highly collaborative board has a very strong culture and is going to outperform one that is not highly collaborative. And I think that's true not just of boards, but also for executive teams, even small teams, and it's a core tenet of Agile, which is what we do at Rally.

Tim Miller, CEO, Rally Software

PROCESS

The process of going public is a complex one that can take 6 to 12 months. In the United States, the SEC governs this process. Most major law firms have a dedicated group to helping companies through an initial public offering (IPO) process.

While there are books that have been written about the details of the process (just ask your lawyer; if he's experienced with IPOs, his firm will likely have written something on it), recognize that the rules are constantly changing. As an entrepreneur, you are fortunate to have lawyers, accountants, and investment bankers who make a living helping companies go public. Use them.

COMMITTEES

We talked about committees earlier in this book. For private companies, especially early on, the entire board will often take on the functions on the individual committees. However, as the company—and the board—gets larger and more mature, it makes sense to create a formal committee structure.

As you begin the process of becoming a public company, you should have at least three committees: compensation, audit, and nominating. Each committee should have a formal charter with their responsibilities clearly spelled out. In addition, each committee should have at least three independent, nonmanagement board members on it. One of these independent members should be the chair of the committee and responsible for coordinating all of the activities of the committee.

CONFIDENTIALITY

As with a sale of a company, confidentiality matters in the context of an IPO. However, in addition to typical confidentiality dynamics, IPOs have a special type of confidentiality called a *quiet period*. This period begins when the company files its first draft of a registration statement and ends when the SEC declares the registration effective. However, there are many nuances and vagaries around the timing, including a more conservative view by many lawyers that the process should start at the first "organization" (or "org") meeting. Furthermore, in 2005 the SEC relaxed the quiet period rules in some situations.

In the United States, the JOBS Act of 2012 introduced a new concept often referred to as a *confidential filing*. In this situation, companies can now file their draft registration statement confidentially and have it remain so until as few as 21 days before the company commences with a road show to sell its securities to the public.

In any of these situations, the board needs to be very involved in the process and very aware of the dynamics around confidentiality. A violation of any of this can jeopardize the entire IPO process.

INSIDER STATUS

After a company goes public, board members will be deemed *insiders*. They will be subject to the same confidentiality and stock trading rules of any other executives in the company. As insiders, they have a particularly high standard of confidentiality and duty of care.

VCs ON PUBLIC-COMPANY BOARDS

Some VCs like to serve on public-company boards; others, such as Brad, don't. There is no industry-wide best practice, and each VC firm will have its own rules and desires. Make sure you know what your VC thinks about public-company board participation well before you go public in order to avoid being surprised.

VCs stay on public-company boards for the following reasons:

- The VC simply enjoys being on the board and the public-company status does not change that dynamic.
- The VC enjoys the "prestige" of being on a public-company board.
- The VC believes that he will continue to expand his own experience and knowledge base being on the board.
- The VC has been persuaded by company management to stay on the board.

VCs leave boards before the IPO for the following reasons:

- The VC is not an expert at dealing with public-company compliance issues.
- The VC doesn't want the fiduciary duties of a public-company board member.
- The VC doesn't want to be restricted from distributing or selling stock that it holds of the company, which is much harder to do when one is a board member and has insider information.
- The VC is worried about the amount of litigation present for the average public company and doesn't want to be involved in lawsuits.
- The VC is in the business of investing and managing early-stage companies, and the VC's investors don't want him using his time managing a company in which he is working to liquidate his position now that it is public.

CHAPTER EIGHTEEN

GOING OUT OF BUSINESS

Unfortunately, many companies are not successful and the business enters a bankruptcy or wind-down process. This situation is one of the most difficult ones for a board to navigate, and the one thing to be certain of is that you have extremely competent legal counsel to guide you through every step of the process. While cash is certainly tight at this point in time, investing some of the remaining cash in strong legal counsel and following their guidance is a wise long-term move. If you don't, in addition to the company's generating additional liabilities, directors may end up being personally liable for mistakes the CEO and the board make.

We discussed the fiduciary duties a board and the board members have to the company and the shareholders earlier in this book. We also discussed how some board members have additional duties to others, such as a venture capitalist having duties to his firm's limited partners. When a company begins to fail, the fiduciary duties of the board can change. Given that these duties are defined by state law and are different from state to state, we'll try to give you a general idea of how this works. But, as with everything else in this section, please do not rely on this book for legal advice. Make sure you have a great lawyer.

THE ZONE OF INSOLVENCY

A *solvent* company is one that has cash to pay for its liabilities and financial obligations. If you have an MBA or were a finance major, you'll start thinking about cash flow versus balance sheet solvency, but for this book, let's keep it simple and say, "If you can pay all your bills, you are solvent."

When a company begins running low on cash, the board must determine whether the company is in the *zone of insolvency*. In layman's terms this means the company is getting close to being insolvent. The zone of insolvency, from a legal perspective, includes three tests:

- Liabilities exceed assets on the balance sheet.
- There is not enough cash available to pay the bills.
- The total amount of cash is unreasonably low.

These tests depend on interpretation and cannot be viewed in isolation. At most startups it's normal to have small amounts of cash in the bank, especially prior to raising a round of financing.

While in the zone of insolvency, some jurisdictions impose additional duties and liabilities on the board of directors. Failure to recognize this and adhere to the additional duties can, depending on state law, lead to personal liability to board members.

When a company is either in or getting close to the zone of insolvency, it's imperative that the board is meeting often. Sometimes this means a weekly or even daily call to monitor the company's financial health. Having your attorney record the minutes during such meetings is critical.

RESPONSIBILITY TO CREDITORS

Normally, state laws don't impose fiduciary duties on boards to creditors. Don't think of creditors as just banks loaning money, but any liability the company has. This includes employees, landlords, your local caterer, your Internet service provider, and the company that is leasing you a copier.

This all can change once the company enters into the zone of insolvency. Some states impose a fiduciary duty to all "stakeholders," not just shareholders at this point. This means that the board owes fiduciary duties to any party with a financial interest in the company, which includes all creditors and employees.

Practically, this means that the board must consider all stakeholders' interests when making business decisions. Should the company spend some money to continue building version two of the product, or should they be paying off their creditors? Should the company hire a new engineer that could help lead to a new customer sale, or should they pay off their copier lease?

What normally ends up happening is that if the board believes that the value to the company is increased by investing in the business, then the company will continue to hire, spend on research and development, or invest in sales. These decisions should be memorialized in the minutes of the meetings. If the board isn't sure, then the company should do its best to preserve assets to pay off creditors.

RESPONSIBILITY TO SHAREHOLDERS

Technically, the board's duties don't change with respect to shareholders during these difficult times. That being said, if the company is severely under water the value of the equity may be zero, which means the board is really working to pay off the creditors of the company. While certainly not a legal duty, the creditors, in practice, are taking priority over the shareholders.

What gets interesting, from a board perspective, is how to treat employees. For instance, if there is an acquihire situation whereby the creditors are made whole and the employees find good jobs at the expense of the shareholders receiving nothing, is the board allowed to approve such a deal? Should the board push back to get a return for the shareholders by carving out some proceeds from the creditors or employees?

Sticky situations can also arise when insider VCs offer a bridge loan to the company, which, instead of a bridge to next financing, leads to insolvency. In this situation, the board, the note holders (or creditors), and the equity holders can overlap into a messy amalgamation. Having at least one outside director in the mix in this situation is important, as it provides an independent voice to support the specific transactions.

There is no legal treatise that will support what happens in reality. VCs should know how risky their investing is. For a VC, getting pennies back on dollars invested doesn't materially impact returns. Generally, reputable VCs will prioritize creditors and employees above their own self-interests in this situation. Because of that, the VC board member will generally also support an outcome that pays off creditors and creates a good situation for employees, at the expense of the shareholders (including them) receiving proceeds.

One last point to consider in the priority analysis is the role of venture banks—banks that specifically exist to loan money to high-risk companies behind VC investments. VCs like to have good relationships with banks in order to get their companies financed. VCs, who are playing for the long-term, will want the bank to get paid back in this scenario so that their future portfolio companies will not be negatively impacted.

LIABILITY

Normally, board members don't run the risk of personal liability as long as they comply with their fiduciary duties. This is generally the case even in wind-down situations, but there are exceptions.

Once again, make sure you have a good lawyer by your side. Personal liability issues are controlled by state law, which changes more frequently than federal law. Depending on where you incorporate and where your company operates, you may need to comply with the laws of both states, which are not always in alignment. Furthermore, if you aren't in the United States, or have foreign operations, this gets even more complicated.

When handled incorrectly, a wind-down can result in individual board members being liable for paying wages owed to employees, for laying off too many people at a particular time, or from creditors who were able to convince a jury that they should have been paid before the board decided to give severance to employees about to be laid off. We've even seen situations where employees were liable for money received that creditors claimed should have gone to them instead.

If board members resign or approve "fraudulent transfers" (for example, paying shareholders dividends) under such circumstances, they are liable for breaching their duties to the corporation.

CHAPTER 11

If things cannot be turned around and there is no soft landing sale, then some form of bankruptcy is likely in your company's near future. Bankruptcies can be elected by the board of directors or, in some cases, imposed on you by nervous creditors who want the assets of the company to be protected by the court.

Chapter 11 bankruptcies are not "going out of business" bankruptcies. Rather, these are reorganizational bankruptcies that normally pay off creditors less than what they are owed and allow the company to continue operations. When you hear about a large airline or car company "going bankrupt," that is exactly what this is. You can still buy a car or fly on a plane, and the plan is that the company will restructure its balance sheet, extinguish large parts of its debt, and continue to operate.

These types of bankruptcies are extremely rare in the startup world, although they do happen with more substantial startups that have a lot of debt in their capital structure.

CHAPTER 7

Chapter 7 bankruptcies are the "going out of business" type. In this situation, the company's assets are liquidated under court supervision, and the company is dissolved. The company will cease to exist after a Chapter 7 bankruptcy. Once again, these can be commenced by a board vote, or in some cases, forced on you by creditors.

They are usually expensive, take a lot of time, make more money for the lawyers than the creditors, and are a stain on a board member's resume. If you are later part of a public offering, you'll have to disclose that you were on the board of a company that went bankrupt. If your company isn't massively messed up, you may be able to avoid a Chapter 7 bankruptcy with an assignment for the benefit of creditors, but if the company is a financial mess with a board that can't agree on what to do and the specter of personal liability is hanging around you, the company may have no choice but to file for Chapter 7 bankruptcy.

ASSIGNMENT FOR THE BENEFIT OF CREDITORS

In general, a much preferable wind-down option to a Chapter 7 or Chapter 11 bankruptcy is an *assignment for the benefit of creditors*, also known as an ABC. It is faster; cheaper; benefits creditors, employees, and shareholders more than lawyers; and doesn't become part of one's resume. Also, it's nearly as safe from a liability standpoint if you choose a qualified company to guide you through the process.

An ABC is a process where the company assigns all the assets and liabilities to a third-party service provider, who works out deals with creditors and winds down the company. At the time of the assignment, all board members cease to be board members and have no further fiduciary duty liabilities. Going forward, the service provider takes over all management and board-level duties. In short, if they screw up during the wind-down period, it's their problem, not yours.

Generally, good ABC service providers make sure the employees are taken care of to the best of their ability, the creditors are made as whole as possible as they sell the remaining assets (everything from office chairs to intellectual property), and the legal entity is wound down.

We've used this process many times, and we much prefer this route over Chapter 11 or Chapter 7 both as board members and as investors.

CHAPTER NINETEEN

CONCLUSION

B oards of directors are complex and dynamic creatures. Our objective in writing this book was to empower the entrepreneur with information about how to create and use a board effectively.

Most board members strive to help and are eager to positively impact a startup's trajectory. However, the group dynamics of a board are often dictated by legal, psychological, and ceremonial practices, some of which are outdated or ineffective.

In laying the groundwork of an effective board, we hope you now have a deeper understanding of the functioning of a board of directors, appreciate the best practices, and can avoid the worst. Managing communications and making decisions effectively, in good times and bad, are two critical elements of a board dynamic. Proactively picking the best board members is like assembling the members of a band—the music can be awesome, if done right.

We hope that investors, especially those who serve on startup boards, can draw upon some of the best practices we discuss. Few formal classes on "how to be a great board member" exist and many investors learn by observing others. At times, bad behavior and patterns get promulgated to new board members since they often don't have the experience or appropriate reference points. Other times, groupthink or herd-behavior takes over, hurting the development of the business.

We wanted to write a book that fills this gap—a book we would have loved to read ourselves when we started our own companies or served on our first boards. Hopefully, this book will help you on your startup journey.

APPENDIX

CHECKLIST 1

PREPARING YOUR BOARD PACKAGE

While there is no standard format for a board package, remember that the goal of the board meeting is to focus on a robust discussion about key topics. As a result, the board package that is sent out in advance should be comprehensive and well organized. Depending on the stage of your company, the "reporting" section of the board package may be more product and technology oriented (as it would be in an earlier-stage company), may be skewed more toward sales and business development (if your company is at the critical go-to-market stage), or may emphasize financial reporting (for a more mature company).

Examples of sections of a typical board package include:

Company financials. It's typical to present prior-month, quarter-to-date, and year-to-date actual financials (profit-and-loss [P&L], balance sheet, and cash flow statement) as well as comparisons to your budget. Also include a rolling 12-month P&L and an accounts receivable (A/R) aging summary. Some board members prefer to get company financials in Excel format (in addition to what's included in the board package) so that they can play around with the data.

Financial performance guidance. Provide guidance for the next month, quarter, and remainder of the year. Being able to project your company's financial performance obviously requires a certain level of maturity in your business, but this is a good way to make sure that financial reporting isn't only about looking in the rearview mirror.

Key operating metrics. These are the nonfinancial metrics you and your executive team use to judge how the business is doing. These include user adoption metrics, user engagement numbers, and cost of customer acquisition. It's easy to include reams of metrics, but which ones actually matter? How is the company doing relevant to expectations? How do they impact the strategic decisions of the company?

Sales and business development pipeline. Include an accompanying narrative on which deals were won, which deals were lost and why, where and why sales efforts are stalling out, and what progress has been made on key deals.

Product/technology development updates. While it's easy to get lost in extensive product road maps, a high-level overview that you come back to regularly, along with demos, is a powerful way to keep the board updated on your product progress.

Administrative and HR updates. Current head count by department; hiring plans for the upcoming month, quarter, and year; as well as any substantive issues or concerns around human resources (HR).

Current capitalization table. It may seem redundant to include a cap table in each board package when a company's capitalization typically doesn't change frequently, but remember that many of your board members sit on multiple boards and work with a lot of companies. Since capitalization often plays an important role in a lot of early-stage company discussions (such as upcoming financing discussions and option grants), it's helpful to just get in the habit of including it in every board package.

CHECKLIST 2

CONDUCTING YOUR BOARD'S ANNUAL ASSESSMENT

Performing an annual assessment of your board, including 360-degree assessments of each board member, is a powerful tool. While some board members can handle this being done in a casual setting, using a facilitator who does all the interviews, consolidates all of the information, and then provides a written evaluation of the board can be very powerful, especially in situations where there is conflict on the board. You get special bonus points for using this same facilitator to do a 360-degree review of the CEO, which would include a direct review by each board member as well as each of the CEO's direct reports.

If you choose not to use a facilitator, following are some topics to consider for the evaluation of the lead director as well as each board member.

LEAD DIRECTOR

- *Leadership.* Aligns differing agendas without letting the meeting get out of hand.
- *Communication.* Ensures that no one board member throws the meeting off track—softens the aggressive and draws out the passive. Offers proactive feedback to the CEO.
- *Decisiveness.* Listens to all points of view and leads the discussion to conclusions.

- *Attitude.* Advocate of the company, focuses the group on positive action, eliminates any emotional poison, gossip, and distraction.
- *Punctuality.* Keeps meetings on the clock.

BOARD MEMBERS

Overall Involvement
- Understands duty of care and duty of loyalty
- Maintains a high degree of accountability to the company
- Understands legal, financial, and regulatory frameworks
- Maintains confidentiality

Engagement
- Attends and participates in meetings
- Reads and reviews material in advance
- Responds in a timely manner
- Reliable and involved during challenging situations
- Able to mentor the CEO

Communication
- Proactive versus reactive
- Honest, timely, and relevant feedback
- With other board members
- With CEO
- With management

Functional Involvement
- Sales
- Marketing
- Finance
- Committee activity

CHECKLIST 3

QUESTION FOR YOUR LEGAL COUNSEL

We've mentioned numerous times throughout this book the value of excellent legal counsel. Experienced startup legal counsel understand their role well and should be able to give you satisfying answers to the following questions:

- Will they attend all board meetings for free or a discounted rate?
- Will they maintain all corporate records?
- Who is the primary customer for the legal counsel—the company, board, or CEO?
- Will they advise the CEO on appropriate matters in managing the dynamic between the board, investors, and CEO?
- Will they advise the board on governance matters, especially situations where the board and their financial interests as investors may diverge?
- Will they participate in an annual board performance review?

CHECKLIST 4

SHOULD YOU GET DIRECTORS AND OFFICERS INSURANCE?

n the process of conducting board duties, numerous decisions have to be made. Directors aim to function with transparency and conduct their affairs in the most diligent manner, yet certain outcomes can lead to lawsuits. It's an occupational hazard.

Directors and officers (D&O) insurance offers protection to the board of directors and the corporation's officers. Insurance pays for defense costs and can cover some or all damages. Early-stage (pre-revenue/product development) startups should aim to procure at least a $1 million coverage, which typically costs $5,000 per year. As the company matures, these amounts should be revisited.

Issues may arise from existing shareholders who believe that the directors did not act in the interest of all shareholders or get appropriate approvals. In certain situations where the corporation fails to meet its federal or state obligations such as taxes, environmental safety, or occupational health, the government can initiate action against the corporation. Former employees can potentially sue directors for a variety of reasons.

Corporations indemnify their directors and officers through bylaws. This is the first line of defense for both your board of directors and your officers. Indemnification includes expenses (including attorney's fees), judgments, fines, settlements, and other amounts actually and reasonably incurred in connection with any proceeding, arising by reason of the fact that such person is or was an agent of the corporation.

However, startups are generally cash constrained, and any legal action will have an impact on already scarce cash resources. As a result, the second line of defense is a strong D&O insurance policy. Such a policy helps preserve corporate funds. In certain situations, corporations become insolvent and yet have lawsuits lingering on. In these situations, D&O insurance becomes the only source of your legal defense funds.

D&O policies will have a number of variables, including scope of coverage, the annual premium, deductibles, limits on the maximum amount covered, and the term of coverage. As with any insurance policy, you should negotiate carefully with several vendors. At the minimum, make sure you understand what the policy covers with regard to the following:

- Director and officer wrongdoings, within specific terms. The policy definition of "wrongful acts" needs to be understood clearly by each director. Fraud or criminal conduct may be obvious; however, negligent acts or "intentional harm" can fall into the subjective category. Minor changes in policy language can have a significant impact on costs.
- The cost of indemnifying directors and officers.
- Defense costs only or defense and damages? Watch for limits and exclusions. The broader the coverage combined with limited exclusions translates to a high premium.
- Exclusions mean what is not covered by the insurance policy. These include misconducts, blatant fraudulent acts, willful breaches of laws, or criminal conduct. In addition, certain exclusions can eliminate coverage when one director sues another or the corporation sues the director.
- Selection of counsel. In some situations, the D&O insurance company has the right to select defense counsel. This is similar to your car insurance company picking the shop that can conduct the repairs to your car when you have an accident. The conflicts in this situation should be managed carefully.
- Process of filing claims, approving defense expenses, or conditions of denial of coverage need to be understood clearly.
- Make sure that corporation's *general liability coverage* insurance policy does not duplicate the coverage with D&O. It's easy to get overinsured and pay too much when your insurance broker is eager and not acting in your best interest.

An insurance broker will identify the insurance provider and offer a quote. Your board should be actively involved in studying the various options and the selection of an insurance carrier. Do not change the coverage or let the policy lapse without input from your board.

CHECKLIST 5

STOCK OPTION GRANTS AND 409A VALUATION

Your board approves all stock options. The value of stock options needs to be ascertained at different points in time. When you grant stock options to employees, the option grant includes the number of shares, vesting period, and the exercise price. A key part of determining the exercise price is coming up with the "fair market value" (FMV) of the common stock underlying the option.

Based on Section 409A of the Internal Revenue Code, there are three ways a company can determine the FMV of its common stock.

1. *Board approval.* The company board determines the FMV. If an option holder gets audited and the IRS thinks the strike price is not the FMV but instead was artificially low, the option holder has burden of proof to show otherwise. In this situation, the option holder will ask for justification of the FMV from the company. While this used to be standard practice, since new 409A rules were enacted in 2005, this approach has generally stopped being used.

2. *Internal expert.* A person internal to the company who has "significant knowledge and experience or training in performing similar valuations" can create a written valuation report detailing the FMV of the common stock. If an inquiry from the IRS occurs, that person's knowledge, experience, and training could all come under question. Thus, this internal expert option has its own challenges.

3. *Outside consultant.* An independent, qualified, experienced valuation firm is hired to create a written valuation report. Voila—the IRS and the accounting industry just helped create a new cottage industry! When you use this option, the IRS has the burden of proof to show the valuation was "grossly unreasonable," which is an almost impossible standard to meet. As a result, this is the best, and most common, option used.

Assuming you are using an outside consultant to do the 409A valuation, this consultant will gather financial and financing information, prepare a lengthy report using numerous valuation methodologies, and conclude with a fair market value for the common stock. The valuation takes into account a number of data points, including:

Company. Assets, debts, capital structure, preferred stock characteristics (its dividends, antidilution, liquidation preferences), warrant coverage, and common stock holdings.
Performance. Net present value of future cash flows or discounted cash flow and liquidity horizon.
Market. Comparable transactions along with discounts for lack of liquidity.

The valuation consultants use industry standard guidelines such as the American Institute of Certified Public Accountants (AICPA) guidelines. These guidelines minimize the voodoo elements of valuation and follow a set of well-defined formulas.

In 2005, when the new 409A rules appeared on the scene, there were no qualified valuation firms. Today, there are many independent firms as well as specialized groups within virtually every accounting firm. When evaluating one, consider the following questions:

- *Experience.* How many valuation engagements have been conducted in the past 12 months? 36 months? Have these engagements been in the relevant stage and sector of your startup?
- *Industry knowledge and breadth.* How many years of experience do the lead professionals have in relevant sectors? Does the firm have a large number of professionals in its valuation department?
- *Competency.* Was the firm's valuation methodology developed using a comprehensive set of data points? Is the report generated using software models, or does it blend art and science, including

market trends, expertise, and authoritative knowledge of the relevant data points?

- *Quality.* Have any of their valuations been determined "grossly unreasonable" by IRS? By company auditors? Have they redone any valuations due to errors? Who bears financial liability if their numbers don't hold up and extend the audit process? Has the firm been directly or indirectly involved in any IRS penalties?
- *Costs.* Are the costs comparable to market?
- *Speed.* How long does it take to do the analysis?

As with any professional service provider, speak with several of their clients for references. Also, check with other CEOs, especially those in similar-stage companies, to see whom they recommend. Finally, if you have a VC investor, it's likely they will have a favorite 409A valuation firm.

It's important that you be involved in the process before presenting the 409A analysis to the board. Along with your chief financial officer (CFO) or VP of finance, go over the analysis in detail with the 409A valuation firm. It's easy for the valuation firm to miss critical data, especially the first time they do the analysis. For example, if the valuation firm forgets to take into account liquidation preferences of the preferred stock when considering common stock payouts, the FMV could be off by as much as 75 percent.

You need to do a new 409A valuation at least once a year. If you have a financing or other corporate event that impacts the company's capitalization or fundamental value, such as the acquisition of another company, you should do a new 409A analysis immediately.

NOTES

CHAPTER 1

1. Joseph Schumpeter, an economist, coined the term *creative destruction* to describe the forces of entrepreneurship and innovation. Growth occurs out of the destruction of previous economic order. As Brad likes to say, creative construction is really what is happening.
2. Fred Wilson, www.avc.com/a_vc/2012/03/the-board-of-directors-role-and-responsibilities.html
3. Brad Feld and Jason Mendelson, *Venture Deals: Be Smarter Than Your Lawyer and Venture Capitalist* (Hoboken, NJ: Wiley, 2011), 61.

CHAPTER 2

1. Google's "code of conduct" is an excellent example and can be found at http://investor.google.com/corporate/code-of-conduct.html

CHAPTER 3

1. Section 2115 of California General Corporation Law (CGCL). See http://codes.lp.findlaw.com/cacode/CORP/1/1/d1/21/s2115
2. Fred Wilson, http://avc.blogs.com/a_vc/2008/02/thoughts-on-cho.html

3. Steve Blank, http://steveblank.com/2011/06/01/why-board-meetings-suck-%E2%80%93-part-1-of-2/
4. Data from Kaplan and Stromberg, 2003. An interesting paper on the importance of independent directors is authored by Brian J. Broughman, "Independent Directors and Shared Board Control in Venture Finance" (July 18, |2011). Indiana Legal Studies Research Paper No. 1123840. Available at SSRN: http://ssrn.com/abstract=1123840 or doi:10.2139/ssrn.1123840
5. Cisco, http://newsroom.cisco.com/dlls/2007/corp_010407.html
6. Aileen Lee, http://techcrunch.com/2012/02/19/why-your-next-board-member-should-be-a-woman-why-your-next-board-member-should-be-a-woman/
7. "The Tilted Playing Field: Hidden Bias in Information Technology Workplaces." Level Playing Field Institute, 2011.
8. James Surowiecki, *The New Yorker*, May 28, 2012, www.newyorker.com/talk/financial/2012/05/28/120528ta_talk_surowiecki

CHAPTER 4

1. Jeffrey Bussgang, *Mastering the VC Game: A Venture Capital Insider Reveals How to Get from Startup to IPO on Your Terms* (New York: Portfolio, 2010).
2. Scott Maxwell, www.businessinsider.com/the-board-of-directors-dream-team-7-board-roles-every-expansion-stage-company-needs-to-have-2013-1

CHAPTER 5

1. A board represents the interests of all shareholders—preferred as well as common. This responsibility, often described as a "fiduciary duty to all shareholders," creates conflicts and challenges in startups, which are dealt with in the following chapters.
2. There are some exceptions, like 500 Startups, who aspire to make many more than 30 investments per fund as part of their strategy.
3. The internal rate of return on an investment or project is the "annualized effective compounded return rate" or "rate of return" that makes the net present value (NPV as NET $* 1 / (1 + IRR)$ ^ year) of all cash flows (both positive and negative) from a particular investment equal to zero.

CHAPTER 6

1. As CEO, you have an obligation to report certain matters to all shareholders, not just the board, in a timely manner.

CHAPTER 7

1. Steve Blank, http://blogs.wsj.com/accelerators/2013/06/17/steve-blank-dont-give-away-your-board-seats/
2. Mark Suster, www.bothsidesofthetable.com/2009/10/12/should-your-startup-have-an-advisory-board/

CHAPTER 8

1. Mark Suster, www.bothsidesofthetable.com/2010/02/12/running-more-effective-board-meetings-at-startups/
2. "Survey on Governance," McKinsey Quarterly, February 2008. Of the 586 respondents, 378 were privately held companies, making it a relevant sample for the purposes of our discussion.
3. K. Patterson, J. Grenny, R. McMillan, and A. Switzler, *Crucial Conversations* (New York: McGraw-Hill, 2002).
4. Mark Suster, www.bothsidesofthetable.com/2010/02/12/running-more-effective-board-meetings-at-startups/
5. Attorney-client privilege is legal concept that allows certain communications between a client (in this case, the company) and attorney to be kept confidential and nondiscoverable during any legal proceedings.
6. Jeff Bussgang, http://bostonvcblog.typepad.com/vc/2011/04/board-meetings-vs-bored-meetings.html

CHAPTER 9

1. Brad's wife, Amy Batchelor, co-author with Brad of *Startup Life: Surviving and Thriving in a Relationship with an Entrepreneur*, loves Robert's Rules of Order.

Whenever Brad is getting too unstructured about how he interacts with her, she simply invokes Robert's Rules, which always gets him to focus on what is going on around him.

2. Make sure you understand the rules of when something is attorney-client privileged (ACP) and when it isn't. For example, ACP applies only if board members and employees are in the room. A single board observer in the meeting will break ACP.

3. MarkSuster,www.bothsidesofthetable.com/2010/02/12/running-more-effective-board-meetings-at-startups/

CHAPTER 10

1. J. Travis Laster, quoted in *The Economist*, June 2, 2012, www.economist.com/node/21556248

2. Until 2005, private company boards could determine the current fair market value of the common stock of the company. In 2005, the IRS introduced Internal Revenue Code, Section 409A, which changed the rules on how fair market value is determined. To be safe, an outside 409A valuation, done by a qualified firm, has to be done at least once a year.

CHAPTER 11

1. This is also covered in Brad's blog in greater detail. See www.feld.com/wp/archives/2011/07/note-to-ceos-decisions-come-from-you-not-the-board.html

CHAPTER 14

1. Steven Kaplan, www.chicagobooth.edu/capideas/dec05/1.aspx

2. Kara Swisher, http://allthingsd.com/20120507/exclusive-flipboard-ceo-mccue-likely-to-step-down-from-twitter-board-over-potential-future-conflicts-or-closer-cooperation/

3. Arthur Rock, interview by Sally Smith Hughes, 2008–2009, http://digitalassets.lib.berkeley.edu/roho/ucb/text/rock_arthur.pdf

4. Walter Isaacson, *Steve Jobs* (New York: Simon & Schuster, 2011), 318–319.

INTERVIEWS

Following are the people interviewed for this book. We appreciate all the time they spent with us.

Micah Baldwin (Graphicly, CEO)
Scott Bannister (IronPort Systems, co-founder)
Jacques Benkoski (US Venture Partners, partner)
Paul Berberian (Orbotix, CEO)
Rajat Bhargava (JumpCloud, CEO)
Tom Bogan (Greylock, partner)
Jon Callaghan (True Ventures, managing partner)
Dane Collins (AWR Corporation, CEO)
Jim Dai (CalmSee, CEO)
Greg Gottesman (Madrona Venture Group, managing director)
Chris Heidelberger (Nexaweb Technologies, CEO)
Will Herman (angel investor)
Richard Huston (Ohio TechAngels, founder)
Eric Jensen (Cooley LLP, partner)
Josh Kopelman (First Round Capital, partner)
Clint Korver (Ulu Ventures, partner)
Manu Kumar (K9 Ventures, chief firestarter)
Wendy Lea (Get Satisfaction, CEO)
Seth Levine (Foundry Group, managing director)
Scott Maxwell (OpenView Partners, senior managing director)
T.A. McCann (Blackberry, vice president)
Kelly McCracken (Aileron, director of client relations)
Ryan McIntyre (Foundry Group, managing director)
Jason Mendelson (Foundry Group, managing director)
Lesa Mitchell (Kauffman Foundation, vice president—advancing innovation)

Cindy Padnos (Illuminate Ventures, managing partner)
Mike Platt (Cooley LLP, partner)
Tim Petersen (Arboretum Ventures, managing director)
Thomas Porter (EDF Ventures, co-founder)
Andy Rappaport (August Capital, partner)
Christopher Rizik (Renaissance Venture Capital, CEO)
Niel Robertson (Trada, CEO)
Adam Rodnitzsky (ShopperTrak, director of product marketing)
Heidi Roizen (DFJ, venture partner)
William Ruckelshaus (Madrona Venture Group, strategic director)
Chris Rust (US Venture Partners, partner)
Lucy Sanders (National Center for Women & Information Technology, CEO)
Greg Sands (Costanoa VC, managing partner)
Zachary Shulman (Cayuga Venture Fund, managing partner)
Mike Smalls (Hoopla, CEO)
Mark Solon (TechStars, managing director)
Shanna Tellerman (Google Ventures, partner)
Steven Tonsfeldt (O'Melveny & Myers LLP, partner)
Sreeram Veeragandham (Gitega Capital)
Todd Vernon (VictorOps, CEO)
Scott Weiss (Andreessen Horowitz, partner)

Following are people who gave us permission to include content in this book from their blogs.

Aileen Lee (Cowboy Ventures, partner)
Steve Blank (Stanford, consulting associate professor): http://steveblank.com/
Matt Blumberg (Return Path, CEO): www.onlyonceblog.com/
Jeffrey Bussgang (Flybridge Capital Partners, general partner): http://bostonvcblog.typepad.com/
Ben Horowitz (Andreessen Horowitz, partner): http://bhorowitz.com/
Richard Huston (Ohio TechAngels)
Scott Maxwell (OpenView Partners, senior managing director): http://blog.openviewpartners.com/
Mark Suster (Upfront Ventures, partner): www.bothsidesofthetable.com/
Noam Wasserman (Harvard Business School, associate professor of business administration): www.noamwasserman.com/blog/
Fred Wilson (Union Square Ventures, partner): http://avc.com/

BIBLIOGRAPHY

Ariely, Dan, *The Honest Truth About Dishonesty: How We Lie to Everyone—Especially Ourselves* (Harper Perennial, paperback, 2013).

Blank, Steve, *The Four Steps to the Epiphany* (K&S Ranch; 2nd edition, 2013).

Blank, Steve, *The Startup Owner's Manual: The Step-by-Step Guide for Building a Great Company*, 1st edition (K & S Ranch, 2012).

Blumberg, Matt, *Startup CEO: A Field Guide to Scaling Up Your Business* (Wiley, 2013).

Christie, Agatha, *And Then There Were None*, reprint edition (Harper, 2011).

Cialdini, Robert, *Influence: Science and Practice*, 5th edition (Pearson, 2008).

Feld, Brad, and Amy Batchelor, *Startup Life: Surviving and Thriving in a Relationship with an Entrepreneur* (Wiley, 2013).

Feld, Brad, and David Cohen, *Do More Faster: TechStars Lessons to Accelerate Your Startup* (Wiley, 2010).

Feld, Brad, and Jason Mendelson, *Venture Deals: Be Smarter than Your Lawyer and Venture Capitalist*, 2nd edition (Wiley, 2012).

Hseih, Tony, *Delivering Happiness: A Path to Profits, Passion, and Purpose*, reprint edition (Business Plus, 2013).

Lehrer, Jonah, *How We Decide*, 1st edition (Mariner/Houghton Mifflin, 2010).

McRaney, David, *You Are Not So Smart: Why You Have Too Many Friends on Facebook, Why Your Memory Is Mostly Fiction, and 46 Other Ways You're Deluding Yourself*, reprint edition (Gotham, 2012).

Patterson, Kerry, Joseph Grenny, Ron McMillan, and Al Switzler, *Crucial Conversations: Tools for Talking When Stakes Are High*, 2nd edition (McGraw-Hill, 2011).

Wasserman, Noam, *The Founder's Dilemmas: Anticipating and Avoiding the Pitfalls That Can Sink a Startup* (Princeton University Press, 2013).

ABOUT THE AUTHORS

Brad Feld has been an early-stage investor and entrepreneur for over 20 years. Prior to cofounding Foundry Group—a Boulder, Colorado–based early-stage venture capital fund that invests in information technology companies all over the United States—he cofounded Mobius Venture Capital and, prior to that, founded Intensity Ventures. Feld is also a co-founder of Techstars and has been active with several nonprofit organizations. He is a nationally recognized speaker on the topics of venture capital investing and entrepreneurship.

Mahendra Ramsinghani has over 15 years of investment and entrepreneurial experience and has led investments in over 50 seed-stage companies. He helped draft the underlying legislation for a fund-of-funds for the State of Michigan. For his contributions, his immigration to United States was approved under "National Interest." He is the author of *The Business of Venture Capital* (Wiley, 2011). His articles and blogs have been published in Forbes, MIT Technology Review, Thompson Reuters peHUB, and Huffington Post. His educational background includes a BE (Electronics) and MBA (Finance and Marketing) from University of Pune, India.

INDEX

CHAPTER THREE

TELLING THE STORY TO YOUR INVESTORS

Once you've iterated a few times on your Lean Canvas and tested assumptions, you're likely off and running and building your product. Now, as CEO, you can turn your focus to telling the story of your company—the customer, problem, and solution—to your key stakeholders.

In short, you need some kind of a business plan.

THE BUSINESS PLAN IS DEAD— LONG LIVE THE BUSINESS PLAN

The phrase "business plan" conjures images of massive tomes filled with charts and graphs of every variety. Startup business stories come in short bursts rather than dozens of chapters. There are two main constituencies to whom you need to be telling the story at this stage.

First, you need to convince investors to fund the effort. Then you have to articulate how you want your employees to fulfill the problem-solution set you're building so you can start building a company alongside your product. While those stories are similar, they aren't identical. For example, your team is primarily interested in what their work lives are going to look like over the next 18 months, while your investors will want to focus on what the likely return from their investment will be.

These two versions of the story need to be told in two different ways, depending on the audience: 10 to 12 slides for investors and a blueprint document for *how* you'll execute on that plan—your mission, vision, and values—for the team.

The business plan isn't dead. It's just gotten a lot shorter.

THE INVESTOR PRESENTATION

As I wrote in one of my sidebars in *Venture Deals*, "There are only a few key things most VCs look at to understand and get excited about a deal." They are:

- The elevator pitch
- The size of the opportunity
- Your competitive advantage
- Current status and roadmap from today
- The strength of your team
- Summary financials

Some of these details—the problem you're solving, your competitive advantage (or "unfair advantage"), and your summary financials—overlap considerably with details in the "Lean Canvas" I described in the previous chapter, though some are different.

The Elevator Pitch

Start by clearly articulating what problem you're solving and for whom. By now, you should have enough clarity around your big ideas to be able to state them quickly and succinctly. Can't do it? Go back over your notes. Were there a few stumbling points? Spots where either you had difficulty stating your ideas or where the people you were speaking about pushed back? Most likely, a lack of clarity around those specific ideas is holding you back. Take a few steps back, and reconsider them. When you come back to your elevator pitch later, it should be much easier to write.

Your elevator pitch needs to be short and punchy. It needs to fit on one slide. It needs to be something that, unless you're in an incredibly technical niche, is understandable by average people who aren't on your team. Try explaining the problem and solution you're working on to someone outside your business world, like a friend or a relative, in order to refine it.

The Size of the Opportunity

Next, you need to pull some elements from the work you did on your Lean Canvas into one slide. Who specifically is your target audience, and how big is your total addressable market (TAM) and your realistic take of the TAM, based on your initial pricing and competitive landscape? These items will vary considerably depending on your business. The average order for mops and Tilex is going to be considerably lower than what BNP Paribas would pay for a new system to clear its trades. That's why the market opportunity needs to include *both* market size and transaction size. Are you selling a $10 product to 20 million potential customers, or a $10 million solution to 20 potential customers? How many of those potential customers do you have to reach for this plan to work? Where else are they spending money today on similar solutions, or how much is their problem costing them?

Your Competitive Advantage

For this section, you can draw largely from your work on unique value proposition and unfair advantage on the Lean Canvas. Investors tend to get very excited about underdog startups that can show a path to disrupting larger incumbents in proven markets. This is your time to shine on that front.

Current Status and Road Map from Today

When we started Return Path in 1999, most startups didn't have a "current status" slide in their investor presentations. You raised money first and built product later because, for the most part, *you had to*. Today, it is so inexpensive to get prototype products to market that you can do an enormous amount of work on your Lean Canvas—testing hypotheses, validating your market—that investors other than your immediate friends and family *expect* you to have completed before you approach them to raise capital.

This section of the investor presentation then becomes critical. Where are you today, and, more importantly, what have you learned along the way?

Again, since we all know that most initial business ideas are wrong some-how, bring potential investors along for the ride. Where did you start out, what did you test, what did you learn, how did you iterate? This is not a sign of weakness—it's a sign of strength!

Once you describe your current status, you need to articulate the road map from today. You know where you want to be in three years. How are you going to get there from where you are right now? This is one section of the investor presentation that needs to start getting into some details. How will you judge your success over the next year? What milestones and key metrics are you looking to hit? What other hypotheses need to be tested? What roles will you need to hire? What investments will you need to make? When will you launch?

The Strength of Your Team

At the dawn of a startup, your first investors are not investing for cash flow, since the business is likely not profitable. They aren't even investing at a valuation that is a multiple of revenue, since there is usually no significant revenue. They are investing in your idea and your market opportunity as well as your theory about how to prosecute that opportunity, in the early work and learning you've done. They're investing in your story. In short, they're investing in the strength of your team.

Unless your team is 100 percent made up of people with zero busi-ness experience and zero direct experience as a potential customer of the product you're building, you should take this opportunity to show off your talent. Why should the investor give you his or her money? You need to communicate why you'll be a good steward of that investment based on the experience you have as a collective team. The only thing you need to make sure you do in this section is to be 100 percent scrupulously honest. Today, it takes only a couple of clicks of the mouse to check facts on LinkedIn or Google. If you were an actual founder of a company before, say so. But if you worked at a startup as an intern during its founding period, don't pre-tend you were a founder!

Summary Financials

This needs to be the most detailed section of your investor presentation, even more so than your road map from today. Even though, as with all forward-looking plans around a startup, the numbers will be wrong over time (and the further out you get, the more wrong they will be!), it's critical to demonstrate to your prospective investors, and to yourselves, that you understand all of the financial drivers of your business at a detailed level. It's also important to show that you know how to build a financial model and that you understand how to manage a business around cash. Finally, it's important to have a good financial model so you know how much cash you're looking to raise!

On the revenue side, you can draw heavily from your TAM work and from the revenue hypotheses you tested on the Lean Canvas. How many customers will you add or lose each month, and how much will they spend with you?

On the cost side, model out the four main expense items: cost of goods, salaries/benefits, marketing, and capital expenditures (CapEx).

Cost of goods is usually defined as the "raw materials" that go into producing your product, or expenses that are variable with revenue. If you're running a software company, these tend to be things like hosting and bandwidth, credit card processing fees, and sales commissions.

Determining your spending on salaries and benefits starts with a headcount plan. What bodies do you need in what seats, and when, in order to execute your plan? How much will you be spending on health care and payroll taxes? Look at every functional area that's appropriate for your area of business, and map out the resources you have today (if any) against where you are today. If you are missing a functional area and don't know how to plan it, ask for help from an adviser.

Marketing and CapEx will differ dramatically based on the kind of business you're running. But you need to think carefully about all the elements of each, as well as the planning that has to go into making the expenses come to life. If you need to renovate your office or expand to a new location in order to accommodate new hires, you need to give your office manager significant lead time to make arrangements. Don't let the excitement of hiring a new sales team turn into a scramble to find desks and monitors.

Don't let your resource planning stop there. Look at every single line item on an income statement. If you're just starting out, a basic accounting software package can be your guide, as can Google or Wikipedia. From rent to travel expenses, to consultants, to the software your people will be using, your planning needs to include every dime.

Revisiting the Big Classics

When you're developing your business and investor presentation, every year and every situation is different. There is probably a shelf of books for every specific challenge you're facing and it's worth making your way through them when you're trying to get a handle on the specific challenges your company is facing. This is also the time to revisit the big classics: the books that you instinctively reach for every time you're stuck; the ones that defined the way you think about every major problem; the ones that inspired you to take on the challenge of starting a company in the first place.

Market research, stakeholder interviews, and a careful review of the literature on your immediate challenges will help you make many of the small decisions that every strategic plan must encompass. The big classics will remind you to take a step back and situate your plan in a much larger context. My favorites are:

> *Profitable Growth Is Everyone's Business* by Ram Charan
> *The Innovator's Dilemma*, *The Innovator's Solution*, and *Seeing What's Next* by Clay Christensen
> *Good to Great* and *Built to Last* by Jim Collins
> *Purple Cow* and others by Seth Godin
> *The Advantage* by Patrick Lencioni
> *The Goal* and *It's Not Luck* by Eliyahu M. Goldratt
> *Blue Ocean Strategy* by Chan Kim and Renee Mauborgne
> *Crossing the Chasm*, *Inside the Tornado*, and *Escape Velocity* by Geoffrey Moore
> *The Underdog Advantage* by David Morey and Scott Miller
> *Competitive Strategy* and *Competitive Advantage* by Michael Porter
> *Positioning: The Battle for Your Mind* by Al Ries and Jack Trout
> *Hardball* by George Stalk and Rob Lachenauer (also check out "Curveball," Stalk's 2006 follow-up article in the *Harvard Business Review*)

INVESTOR PRESENTATIONS FOR LARGER STARTUPS

Unless you invent not only cold fusion but a model that funds your business without requiring outside capital, you'll go through the process described in this chapter a number of times as you scale up your business. This may seem like a hassle, but it's actually a good thing for you as the entrepreneur in the end. If you have to absorb $20 million in losses before building a profitable business, better to raise the money in chunks at escalating valuations so you minimize dilution. More to the point, it's required, since investors will always want to see you derisk their investment piece by piece over time.

As you get larger and larger, the preceding steps are still relevant as an outline, but the work you do to flesh out the outline has to get more and more detailed. New sections or slides have to be added. Who are some reference customers? How are they using and liking the product? If you lost a couple of customers (or are in a consumer business where you lose lots of customers), why did you lose them? How did actual financials compare to your plan? How specifically will you use the dollars invested in the business? Are your early investors going to put more money in this round?

Virtually every company in the world has investors and shareholders. Learning how to tell your company's story to them is an incredibly important part of running a company. Even if you're a product-oriented CEO, or the company's best engineer, if your title is CEO, you are doing this work yourself. Although a good CFO will participate in this process, especially as you get larger, raising money is the process of selling someone else on your vision of the business and of a world made better by it. This is awfully hard to delegate to someone else.